From Disadvantaged Girls
to Successful Women

From Disadvantaged Girls to Successful Women

Education and Women's Resiliency

Pamela LePage-Lees

Westport, Connecticut
London

Library of Congress Cataloging-in-Publication Data

LePage-Lees, Pamela.
    From disadvantaged girls to successful women : education and
women's resiliency / by Pamela LePage-Lees.
        p.   cm.
    Includes bibliographical references (p.) and index.
    ISBN 0–275–95752–7 (alk. paper)
    1. Socially handicapped women—Education—United States—Case
studies. I. Title.
    LC4091.L47   1997
    371.822—dc21   97–11080

British Library Cataloguing in Publication Data is available.

Library of Congress Catalog Card Number: 97–11080
ISBN: 0–275–95752–7

First published in 1997

Praeger Publishers, 88 Post Road West, Westport, CT 06881
An imprint of Greenwood Publishing Group, Inc.

Printed in the United States of America

The paper used in this book complies with the
Permanent Paper Standard issued by the National
Information Standards Organization (Z39.48–1984).

10 9 8 7 6 5 4 3 2 1

to my loving and supportive husband, David Lees

Contents

Acknowledgements

I would like to give special thanks to the women who volunteered for this project. Their stories made this a truly interesting and rewarding experience. I have nothing but admiration for their perseverance and strength. I would also like to thank Jim Stone, Doris Flowers, Marcelle Kardush and David Lees who provided excellent advice and feedback during the research process. Finally, I would like to thank my colleagues at the Institute for Educational Transformation at George Mason University, especially Hugh Sockett, whose encouragement and understanding enabled me to finish this book by the end of my first year as an assistant professor during which time I also became a new mom.

1

INTRODUCTION

When I was 13 years old, the government gave cheese to low income families. Once a month my mother and I would traipse down to a large auditorium-sized room and pick up a huge brick of American cheese. Well-dressed women from the other side of town would produce a sympathetic smile, hand us our cheese and then pat themselves on the back. These women were graciously giving up their valuable time to help "those" people. I knew some of these good Samaritans. I cleaned their homes on the weekends to make extra money. They were kind women who genuinely wanted to help. For this reason they were truly baffled as people became surly and rude when presented with cheese. Their puzzled faces revealed confusion: Why are these people upset? Why are these people unappreciative? Why are they mad at me? These ladies had very little understanding of how those of us on the other side of the cheese table felt. Even then I wanted to say, "Don't you understand? We don't want your cheese; we don't want your sympathy; we don't want to clean your houses. What we want is to be like you. We want to live in a nice house. We want to wear nice clothes. *We* want to be in a position to help others. We don't want cheese. We want the opportunity to be like you!"

This book is about women who decided many years ago that they did not want free cheese; they wanted instead to make comfortable lives for themselves. My gift to successful women who have faced stress is not a brick of American cheddar, but instead some hope, some advice and some validation. The story in this book is the result of a two-year study to explore the experiences of women who achieved highly in academics and who were also disadvantaged as children. The women were considered high achievers since they had earned advanced degrees or were currently enrolled as advanced graduate students with at least two years of graduate work completed. Women were considered disadvantaged as children if they were raised in low-income homes, were first-generation college students, and had faced stress as children (e.g., family dysfunction or instability, illness, or death, etc.). From this definition, the women's resources had been limited in three categories: financial, informational and emotional.

People rarely explain why some children from disadvantaged backgrounds do well. Even when they do, the family is often credited as being most influential in fostering successful outcomes (Clark, 1983; Gandara, 1995; Gotwalt & Towns, 1986). This explanation did not satisfy my curiosity about resiliency. In many families, one child will do well while his or her siblings do poorly. In fact, two of the women I interviewed for this book had siblings who had committed suicide. The majority of the women whose stories I present here did not have support at home. Often their family life was an obstacle to their success. Nonetheless, they were quite successful. I was curious to find out why.

There are many definitions of resiliency. The term "resiliency" is often used by psychologists to describe people who function at a high level after experiencing numerous stressors. The disagreement centers on what constitutes stress and on how to measure function. For example, a psychologist may describe a child as resilient if he or she had a psychotic parent and later in life has functional relationships. In this book, I do not concentrate on personal relationships. I use resiliency to describe women who overcame barriers and did well in school; however, it is acknowledged that success can be measured in many other ways.

The information I present here was gathered in three ways. I collected personal stories through individual in-depth interviews, questionnaires and school records. The interviews took place in the San Francisco Bay area, although most of the women were raised in different parts of the country, including (but not limited to) California, Massachusetts, New York, Wisconsin, Washington, D.C., and South Carolina (see Appendix A).

MOTIVATION TO WRITE THIS BOOK

I was initially motivated to write this book for two reasons that relate to my personal history. As I mentioned earlier, I was poor when I was a child, but I was also disadvantaged in other ways. For example, I went to 14 different schools in four different states by the time I graduated from high school. My mother was mentally ill and my stepfather was physically abusive. As a very young child, one of my first memories involved being placed in a "children's home." The guardians of that fortress put children into toilets and told them they would be flushed down if they cried or misbehaved. As a teenager I lived with my mother on welfare, and those years were vividly marked by the death of my boyfriend who committed suicide in jail after getting caught burglarizing a restaurant with my brother.

Because of my history, I became interested in reading about the educational experiences of women and disadvantaged children in books and journals. In most cases, my experience was absent. I found that many people have attempted to explain why children from poor backgrounds fail, but when they succeed, they are usually ignored. Those people who do write about poor children rarely write about their own experience with disadvantage. I suspect that most academics have come from a traditional middle- or upper-class childhood. Those who have not hide their backgrounds, which perpetuates the common belief that all academics grow up privileged. Researchers from privileged backgrounds who have studied disadvantaged children have done very well analyzing the experiences of children who grew up in very different circumstances from their own. But I believe they have missed subtle, yet important, aspects of the behaviors they study, and their communication style, along with that of many of their less privileged colleagues, is so jargon ridden and impersonal that it does not reach the people who could make significant changes.

In the last few years we have started hearing more about successful women from disadvantaged backgrounds, but mainly about unusual cases such as young girls who survive foster homes to become Miss Teenage America, or those who kill their mothers and go on to Harvard, or occasionally the ethnic minority woman who becomes the president of a university. There is no recognition that even people who were not involved in beauty contests, matricide or top-level administration can succeed, but in less glorious or notorious ways.

For many years I wanted to stay away from educational issues that were too personal. I was afraid that my colleagues would criticize my subjectivity. I changed my mind as I read stories presented from people who have had firsthand experience with the material they discuss. Many offer insights that I do not find when reading stories presented by outsiders. I now believe that certain groups have been shut out of the academic process because people from the traditional majority subtly communicate that it is inappropriate for people from marginalized groups to reflect on their own experiences. In many ways they suggest that only the "objective outsider" can truly conduct a scientific study. After studying education for 15 years, it is clear to me that there is no way to conduct a completely objective study in social science and that it is important for me to adhere to my beliefs and express my voice honestly. I believe my experiences have provided me with the empathy needed to reflect on disadvantaged women's lives in ways that outsiders cannot.

In many books, the authors are the experts who analyze the experiences of the "subjects." For example, I once read a book about academically successful Hispanic men and women from poor backgrounds. Although the author has a Spanish surname and a Ph.D., I could not tell whether she could have qualified for her own study. She was always the expert, her subjects were always those being studied. In this book, I do not consider myself the expert. The women I interviewed were my peers and often advanced colleagues. Frequently, they gave me interpretations of their own experiences and feedback on my research methods.

I fully admit that my lenses have been shaped by my experiences throughout the years. In some places in this book, I have included my own feelings and experiences alongside those of women represented. Although it was important to me to focus on the voices of the women I interviewed, in reality, my voice is apparent whether or not I pretend to be the objective outsider and present cold, unfriendly, academic prose. I honor the fact that my participants and I were partners in this endeavor, and I feel that an honest dose of reality (something often missing in academics) will provide readers with a better understanding of how my experiences have impacted my interpretations.

I would also like to point out that although my interpretations were influenced by my experiences, I have made an extraordinary effort to accurately represent the women's voices. For example, I sent each volunteer my interpretations of the interviews and asked her whether or not I represented her voice accurately. This feedback was especially important to me because often my explanations went beyond what any one person actually said in her interview. None of the women claimed her voice was misrepresented. In fact, all of the women who responded were very positive. Below I have included some of their comments. All other comments are included in Appendix D.

Maria: I think that my voice was well represented in this study.

Toni: I really enjoyed reading this study. It was interesting and amusing to see myself quoted alongside, within, and among others. Many of your interpretations hit the nail on the head. For example, attitudes described on page... which motivate children and families to hide dysfunction rang true for me.

Janet: In sum, it was validating to read of other women's experiences and to realize there's a whole closet community of us out there. I hope your study can help others.

Helen: Thank you for sending the results of your study. I appreciated hearing what others said and how you interpreted our material. In reading the quotes of the other participants, I found that many things that others said, I could have said too. I think you have done an excellent job of interpreting our material, and I can't say how glad I am to see such a study be done.

No Identification: I was very impressed with how similar my experiences and attitudes were to the other participants in the study, both in terms of the interpretation and the quoted passages.

Sara: I'm really impressed by the study-as I said when you interviewed me, this seems like a really important area of research, and you've done an excellent job!

I wrote this book not only because I thought the stories of high-achieving women from disadvantaged backgrounds were missing or misrepresented. The second reason that I wrote this book was because my journey through school and beyond has been very difficult. I believe that I have given up too much of my life to fulfill a simple dream of helping women and disadvantaged children. At times the emotional strain, the enormous amount of work, and the unremitting pressure that I have had to face was almost too much to bear just so that I could present a voice in women's resiliency. This sentiment has been expressed by many successful women, not only those who have faced the stresses I describe in this book. If our society wishes to encourage women and children from nontraditional backgrounds, we need to change our expectations and our understanding of how people function in various roles. This book was not written from the perspective that people should pull themselves up by their bootstraps. The women in this book were unanimous in their belief that the achievement process was too difficult. They wanted to make the process easier for those who would follow in their footsteps.

So, initially my motivations for writing this book were based on my belief that the literature on women's resiliency is incomplete and that my personal achievement process was too difficult. However, after finishing my interviews, I was motivated for another reason. Before this project, I had assumed that my volunteers would be representative of only a small minority of women in this country. In fact, at the beginning of this project, my colleagues were concerned that I might have trouble attracting participants. My plan was simply to hang flyers on bulletin boards at major universities and hope that qualified women would volunteer. Beyond that, I had three or four backup plans in case I received no calls. To my surprise, within two weeks, I had all the volunteers that I needed and started turning callers away. It was obvious that I had "struck a nerve." Not only did this population seem much larger than I had expected, but the women constantly told me how glad they were that someone was finally paying attention to them. Finally, they had the opportunity to speak their minds. Finally, someone cared about their difficulties. Finally, someone was ready to validate their experiences as women, and women from disadvantaged backgrounds. Although these participants had done well in school, the process had been long and arduous. Also, many other women have come to me since and told me that they could have participated in this project. Once, while I was interviewing for an academic position, the vice-provost of the college told me that she could have been interviewed for my book. Other women have told me that they were qualified under at least two (if not three) of my criteria for disadvantage. I was discouraged to find that many more successful women than I expected had endured stress and poverty as children.

On the other hand, I was happy to find that many women have taken advantage of opportunities. The push for equal opportunity has allowed some people from nontraditional backgrounds to slip through the back door. These women are now starting to find their way into higher-level positions and are struggling to understand how best to function in these positions given their differences. It is hoped that this book not only will help students as they maneuver their way through school, and educators as they find better ways to encourage disadvantaged youth, but also will help those successful people in higher-level positions who believe they must hide who they are to succeed, who feel isolated and different and who question whether their difficulties are the result of their difference or a lack of talent.

While many social scientists have worked diligently over the last 20 years to give voice to certain groups, high-achieving women from disadvantaged backgrounds have been ignored. This oversight has been unfortunate, since the ideas presented by the women in this book are extremely insightful and could assist us in improving education for all students.

2

DESCRIPTION OF THE
PARTICIPANTS

The word "disadvantage" carries with it an interesting history. In the late seventies and early eighties it became unpopular to associate disadvantage with family functioning because it was considered racist. In the past, the word disadvantage has been associated with deficiencies in the child-rearing practices of African-American families. For example, in his book, *The Truly Disadvantaged*, Wilson states: "The controversy surrounding the Moynihan report had the effect of curtailing serious research on minority populations in the inner city for over a decade, as liberal scholars shied away from research behavior construed as unflattering or stigmatizing to particular racial minorities" (Wilson, 1987, 4).

The women of color who were interviewed for this book did not mention the historical abuse of the term "disadvantage," but some of the older white women did. These women claimed that in their school experience, if you were white, you could not be disadvantaged. This attitude stems from our racist history because in the past, Caucasians wanted to believe that they were above the dysfunction they ascribed to ethnic minority families. For a while, disadvantage was synonymous with being deficient, which was also synonymous with being Black. So, to avoid the label of racist and to avoid offending parents, researchers started avoiding variables associated with family functioning. Ultimately, labeling all minority families as being deficient was racist; however, ignoring family problems such as alcoholism and physical abuse invalidates the experiences of those children who are dealing with stress, no matter what their ethnicity. The women of color in this book were suspicious of the term "disadvantage," and the white women were frustrated that although they considered themselves disadvantaged, others were unwilling to validate the interpretation of their own experience.

Today most professionals who write about the disadvantaged use the first few paragraphs to describe their populations (Bempechat & Ginsburg, 1989; Levin, 1985; Fantini & Weinstein, 1968; Slavin & Madden, 1989). Henry Levin (1985) has described the educationally disadvantaged as those children who lack the home and community resources to benefit from conventional school practices. He continues to explain that because of poverty, cultural obstacles or linguistic differences, they tend to have low academic achievement and high dropout rates. He also explains that educationally disadvantaged children are heavily concentrated among minority groups, immigrants, non-English-speaking families and economically disadvantaged populations.

Levin (1985) claims that disadvantaged children tend to have low achievement and high dropout rates, but many other researchers describe disadvantaged children as those who do poorly in school because of lack of resources in either home, school or community. In this project, the women's achievement level was not an indication of whether or not they were disadvantaged (obviously). These women were considered disadvantaged if they faced barriers as children. Ultimately, the women who were considered qualified to participate in this project had these backgrounds in common:

- They lived in either a poor working-class or lower-class family as a child.
- They were first-generation college students.
- They experienced at least one type of familial dysfunction or traumatic childhood stress (physical and or sexual abuse, alcoholism, drug abuse or mental illness, severe illness). A complete list can be found in the Appendix A.

CHARACTERISTICS

Economic Status

When women called to volunteer, I expected more questions about whether or not they encountered stress as children. Actually, there were more questions about socioeconomic status. Providing a precise monetary definition for low, middle or high economic status was problematic because children often do not know the intimate details of their parent's financial situations. Most of the women had no problem describing themselves as being raised in a low-class, working-class or lower-middle-class family. But a few of the women considered themselves middle-class and were not sure if they qualified. In many of these situations, their self-classification was suspicious. For example, one woman labeled herself middle-class even though her father had worked on an assembly line, her mother did not work, and together they raised eight children. In the situations where women were unsure, financial qualifications were discussed in detail and some flexibility was allowed for women who labeled themselves middle-class but whose family obviously faced financial difficulties. If the women had questions about whether or not they were middle- or lower-class, ultimately they were allowed to participate if their parents had experienced some financial difficulties and were unable or unwilling to provide financial support for them in college. A table describing demographic and risk profiles is included in Appendix A.

First Generation College Students

All the women were first-generation college students which is often considered a risk factor in and of itself. Although some of the women's parents may have had some vocational training or attended some junior college classes, if the parents did not finish a four-year degree before their children finished their college degrees, these women were considered first-generation college students. In many cases, the women in this study were the first in their families to graduate from high school.

Childhood Stress

It is important to emphasize that not all the women had parents historically described as dysfunctional. Women were qualified if they had encountered any type of childhood stress. Occasionally, this meant that children had parents who died, others had traumatic experiences with siblings, and some dealt with their own drug or alcohol use.

The women were able to identify types of stress they encountered as children by checking down a list of possible stressors. This list is included in Appendix A. At the bottom of the list, I gave them the opportunity to add any other stressors that were not presented in this list. The stressors that the women checked may have been associated with a parent, a sibling, themselves or a significant other. The women most often focused on one stress. For example, alcoholism was very prevalent in the participants' families. However, many of the women were surprised how many other stressful life events they had endured besides the one main stress that had motivated them to volunteer for this project. By focusing only on the most traumatic events in their lives, many had never reflected on other stress they had encountered as children.

As I mentioned, not all the women had parents (or siblings) they described as dysfunctional; however, discrepancy in attitude between the women was most often associated with the amount and type of stress that these women endured. In other words, many of the women in this study had faced stress associated with parental dysfunction. Some, however, did not. For example, a few women had to face the stress of a parent who was sick and later died. Although this is a tremendous stress, the parents in these families may have been supportive before they died. Also, the one parent who survived may have been supportive and understanding before, during and after the initial trauma. A majority of the women in this book dealt with dysfunctional family interactions.

Diversity

Many research projects have focused on the experiences of wealthy, white, heterosexual, Anglo-Saxon people. For this book, I made an effort to include a diverse group of women. While most volunteers were Caucasian, four of the 21 women considered themselves part of an ethnic minority group. Two were Hispanic and two were African-American. One other participant was Asian-American, but she was the only person who ultimately did not meet the criteria, so her story was excluded from the book. From the remaining group of white women, three of the participants described themselves as being disabled now or in the past. Also, one woman was Jewish and her father had emigrated from Israel. Another participant had emigrated from Germany as an adult. Finally, one woman identified herself as being a lesbian. The participants were also diverse in age. Ages ranged from 24 to 54. Six people were in their twenties, eleven were in their thirties, three were in their forties and one was in her fifties. The largest percentage of women were in their thirties.

Academic Success

As was mentioned in the first chapter, to qualify as high achievers, the women had to have an advanced degree or currently be enrolled as an advanced graduate student with at least two years of graduate work completed. Women were recruited from all disciplines, including education, law, medicine, engineering, business, literature and psychology. The women who volunteered came from social science, humanities, science and business backgrounds. A complete educational profile is included in Appendix A.

Racial Issues

People are often curious to know if there was a significant difference between the Caucasian women and the women of color and also between the young women and the older women. Interestingly, I found less difference between these groups than I expected. Obviously, the women from ethnic minority groups had to deal with an added stress of being part of a group that has been oppressed in our society. Therefore, besides the other disadvantages, these women also faced discrimination and oppression related to race. Also, women of color talked more about barriers associated with peer pressure. If it sounds as though race was underplayed, this may be possible. I believe the women downplayed race. Although race can be a significant barrier for many people, the women in this book did not claim to be seriously affected by racial issues for a number of reasons, including where they grew up as children, their exposure to the white culture, their ability to maneuver gracefully in two cultures and their own experience with race. For example, the most significant racial problem described by the Hispanic women in this book was that in school, their ethnicity was ignored completely. They were never encouraged to appreciate their ethnic origins; instead, they were encouraged to ignore their origins. There was a slight indication that some of the women's attitudes about racial issues were changing. In other words, although they had never thought much about the negative consequences of racism when they were children, as adults who were now competing in the workforce, they were starting to recognize and accept that racism was having more impact than they had allowed themselves to believe in the past. If the women of color did downplay race, this was consistent with the fact that women also downplayed their other disadvantages, and many of them downplayed gender issues. Downplaying disadvantage was a major theme that emerged from my discussions with the women. It seems that adapting and assimilating to a majority style helped the women to succeed.

Age Differences

There were some differences between older and younger women, but not as many as I expected. The largest difference was that the older women were more likely to have their degrees and be working in the field. The younger women were more likely to be still in school. However, that wasn't always true; one woman was 26 years old and already had her Ph.D.

The older women were also more likely to mention sexism. A few of the older women felt that in school they were led to believe that men and women were treated equally, and when they started their careers in business or in academia, they were surprised at the negative impact of sexist attitudes and behaviors. The younger women were more likely to downplay the influence of gender. In my initial interpretations, I thought that the older women may have experienced more difficulties with sexism than younger women. I concluded that the times were changing. When I asked the women for feedback on my interpretations, a few women disagreed with these conclusions. Most of the older women felt that the younger women just hadn't been out there long enough to experience the inevitable. They also felt that younger women were experiencing a type of denial or backlash about sexist attitudes.

There is no doubt that the face of sexism has changed in 30 or 40 years; however, the positive aspects of this change are sometimes exaggerated. For example, the youngest woman in this study (24 years old) claimed that she told a teacher in her elementary school that she was being sexually abused and the teacher ignored her cry for help. This woman graduated from high school in

1987. Often the assumption that "things are different now" is made too quickly. Some of the same problems that existed 40 years ago still exist today. Ideals often change faster than real-life behavior and attitudes.

Marital Status

More than half of the women in this book (12 out of 21) were single. Eleven of the single women had never been married. Two of the single women had college-age children. Six of the participants were currently married. Three of them mentioned that they had children. Three others did not mention whether or not they were involved with significant others or had children. None of the women credited their husbands with their success. Only one woman claimed that her husband supported her financially while she was in graduate school. However, as an undergraduate she supported herself.

A FEW STORIES

The information presented so far in this chapter outlines some basic similarities and differences among the women. However, it is impossible to really get to know these women unless you hear their stories. For that reason, I have chosen five women to represent the larger group. It is hoped that all the women's stories will unfold to some extent throughout the book. Still, I have chosen to highlight five women as examples of the larger group. I chose these particular women because their stories demonstrate the diverse range of ages, occupations, achievement levels, ethnic backgrounds and geographic origins among the women I interviewed. I have presented some parts of their stories in their own voices.

Helen: I was born in Arkansas in a rural area, and I lived there until I moved to Texas. I was married by that time. I was born in '39 so my growing up was in the forties and fifties. I had parents. My father died when I was 17 after being ill with cancer. Yes, I did have siblings. Actually the family was kind of a complicated family. I always like to think of it as three families because my parents were both married previously. Both of them had been widowed, and they both had children before they married each other. My father's children were considerably older. My father was 20 years older than my mother and so his children were, when they married, almost out of the home. He had a large family. This is part of what our difficulty was—there were so many children in the family. My mother also had children, and they were considerably younger. I was one of the third family. The third family had six children, and three of the children died in infancy. I was in the midst of this. There were two children who were older than I who died. Then the one who came right after me, who also died. So I was really isolated by the fact that all these children had died in infancy around me. You have to understand that this was in the thirties. My parents married in 1935, so this was a period where depression was really serious and the family was threatened by starvation. So I'm not surprised that they died.

Helen is a Caucasian woman who was raised in Arkansas. She is now in her 50s, has a Ph.D. in the social sciences, and works as a full professor and department head at a prestigious university. Helen claimed that she was disadvantaged because of the severe poverty that her family endured, especially during the depression. Although poverty was pervasive in her mind, as Helen described her disadvantages, she was surprised how many other stresses she had actually encountered as a child along with her poverty. Her father was an alcoholic and died when she was young. Her mother did not believe in schooling and often set up barriers to her achievement. After working for many years as a secretary when she was a young woman, Helen went to a junior college at night and was given a scholarship to go to a prestigious university as an undergraduate. After her undergraduate degree, Helen went on to get a Ph.D., also from a well-known university.

Joy: I started out growing up in East Boston, Massachusetts, which is lower-income, Irish, Italian Americans of the time. My father has, I think, a fourth-grade education—conceivably a seventh-grade education, but did not graduate high school. He had to quit school on and off to rake blueberries. My father is the perfect example of Bill Cosby's "We ate dirt and we were grateful." He walked five miles uphill to school, both ways, in the snow, with no shoes. I mean, he has every story in the world.

My mother went to, not secretarial school, but some sort of two-year thing. It wasn't an associates. She got a certificate, but it was basically JC—to be a bookkeeper—not an accountant, but a bookkeeper. She had me when she was 20, so my father was 24.

My dad is a mechanic, and he's a biker, or used to be a biker. Him and his brothers started a gas station and eventually each started their own gas station, and my father made a ton of money as a young man. When I was seven, we moved to New Hampshire, big 13-room ranch house. I was a snotty little rich kid in the middle of the woods, and I thought this was going to be very boring.

I went from being lower-income to wealthy for a very short period of time, and only wealthy in comparison to our neighbors because we moved to the boondocks. And then my father was injured. He was underneath a car. He was working for somebody else just part-time, and a car engine fell out on top of him, and he caught it in like a moment of panic and threw it aside and got a hernia and also burst multiple vertebras. Then he had multiple operations, and they cut a nerve by accident, so he has no feeling on the left side of his body. And then they gave him steroids to make his muscles stronger to support what his bones no longer could, and that gave him angina, and he had a massive heart attack. Only a third of his heart works now. He has to wear nitroglycerin at all times— belly-jelly, we call it. He's had multiple heart attacks over the years, and he's been disabled since, I guess, he was 30-something.

So I went from being the street-smart street kid to the little princess, to deeply impoverished where the state was paying our house taxes so we didn't lose the house, and my mother had 15 jobs and I was baby-sitting my brother. I was 10 and my brother four when this all came down.

Joy is a Caucasian 28-year-old doctoral student in the social sciences. She attended numerous colleges as an undergraduate. She went to Harvard as a master's degree student and was attending a well-known university in California as a doctoral student. Joy has had many adventures in her twenties, including a job in the Peace Corps. In the Peace Corps, she worked for many years in Tunisia and was proud that she had made some strides toward improving education for disabled children and adults in that country.

Maria: I was born in Oakland. My dad is a Mexican national and my mom is a Mexican American, second generation. And they met, got married, I was born, and then my younger sister was born, who's two and a half years younger than I am, and we lived here for about four years after I was born, and then we moved to Mexico. My mom had never lived in Mexico, so she was basically an American girl going to another country with her two kids, but she was following her husband. We lived there for about eight years, and my experience is really cross-country because we lived there during the school year and then came up here during the summertime and spent all summer with my maternal grandparents. We lived just across the border in a very small town close to Tiajuana. It's really small, I mean tiny, cobblestone, really little; and my dad was self-employed and did like cabinetry work. So he had his own business, which, you know, sometimes it went well and sometimes it didn't go well. My mom worked. My mom always worked. She's always done, not secretarial, but more bookkeeping, accounting. So, yeah, definitely had an experience of being-you know, having both working parents. It was a difficult childhood. I told you that my dad is an alcoholic and was probably an alcoholic since I was 12. That was just what he grew up in, so that pervades my memories-I mean, the fact that my dad was an alcoholic. He was also an abusive person towards my mom-not towards us, but towards my mom. So I grew up with all of that turmoil.

Maria is a 26-year-old Hispanic woman who graduated from a prestigious university where she earned an undergraduate degree in business. She received a master's in public administration. When she was a child, her parents eventually got divorced, and she moved with her mother and sisters to a rural town in California. At that time, her mother supported her and her two sisters by working as a bookkeeper. Maria had very positive things to say about her mother's commitment to her children. All three of the daughters in her family went on to become successful young women who graduated from prestigious universities. One is an engineer, one is now in college, and Maria is a successful businesswoman. All three daughters are involved in occupations that are nontraditional for women.

Toni: I'm the youngest of eight children. I grew up in northern Indiana, which is sort of a real steel mill area. My grandfather was a steel mill person, my father was a steel mill person, all my brothers worked in the steel mill, and my mother was just a housewife. She went to high school, though. It was kind of a big deal because she had to drop out of high school during the depression—but she went back to high school and finished. That was kind of a big deal for her. My father finished high school, too. The family was kind of complex because my mother was married to someone who died in World War II and they had a couple of children; then she remarried my father, who had three children, and then when they got married they had three more children. So it was a kind of complex stepfamily. I was the youngest of them all. My father was a nicotine addict; he was like a chain smoker. While I was growing up he was like dying of emphysema, and he died when I was 15. My mother died of breast cancer when I was 20.

Toni is a 30-year-old Caucasian doctoral student in biology. She went to a well-known midwestern college as an undergraduate and was earning her Ph.D. from an East Coast Ivy League university. Toni credits her undergraduate mentor for her success, but is disappointed with the guidance she received in graduate school. Since Toni's parents died by the time she was 20, she has felt alone and on her own for many years. During the interview, she talked about how difficult it had been to go to school for so long while knowing she had no parental backup in case of failure.

Janus: Was I disadvantaged? I guess disadvantaged in the sense that if you had seen me in high school, I was probably the kid that you would have said was not going to—go to school—to make it. I was probably that kid. I always say that I am that statistic—I could easily have been that child—I got pregnant at a very early age and I could have been a statistic for a welfare mother or whatever. I guess I'm supposed to be on welfare right now, I don't know. I could easily have been that statistic if my mother wasn't there to say, well, we understand this mistake now. If I didn't have teachers there saying, well—it doesn't mean you have to stop school. It's not that I didn't have it within myself to learn and to be a productive citizen and contribute to our society. I always thought that would happen. It's just that I was doing all the things that I think you would not do if you wanted—to go to college. That in addition to nobody in my family had ever gone to college. My mother had started college, and I got a lot of inspiration from her. I just assumed I would go to college because I wanted to in some weird way—I don't know. Our family was-well we were very poor, so we didn't even think along those lines, and certainly my father didn't think along those lines. I was not brought up in a family where you would think that I would—normally progress. And I was the first one to actually graduate from high school. Since then—I have a younger sister and she's gone to college and graduated, and a lot of my older sisters and brothers started to go back because they had dropped out of high school. So they started to go back to get their GEDs or whatever and then pursue other careers. So I think the disadvantage—I think the chance or the opportunity is there, I just don't think we have the right equipment to pursue it actively. So to that I would say that I'm still disadvantaged.

Janus is an African-American woman in her middle 30s who was raised in a poor urban area. She had a child at 17 years old, and her mother helped her care for her child while she progressed through school. Janus credits her mother for her success and tells a story about how her mother once put a worm in her hand and told her not to fear things. Although her father was an abusive alcoholic, Janus found ways to ignore his faults and take advantage of the positive aspects of his personality. She was the first of eight children to go to college and is now an associate professor in a technical area in the social sciences.

Every woman who chose to participate in this project had an interesting story to tell. One woman had been involved in the administration of a local Catholic church for many years, and after fighting a number of battles with sexism and conservatism, she left the church. Today she is finishing a Ph.D. in the humanities and is interested in women's spirituality.

Another woman was born and raised in West Germany and provided a comparison of her educational experiences in Germany and the United States. Another women spent years in Israel, where she was educated at the Hebrew University. She followed her dream of going to Israel even though her family did not practice Judaism. Another woman described her fascinating journey to become an architect.

After hearing the women's stories, I was thoroughly impressed and wondered how much of their unique lives had been hidden. For some of these women, I was the first person who had heard their incredible stories. As you will find later, many of them believe that they achieved highly because they were able to successfully hide their backgrounds.

3

PERSONALITIES OF RESILIENT WOMEN

Certainly the women in this book faced stress as children, but did they have personalities that made them immune to the effects of a stressful lifestyle? Many would like to believe that resilient people are never truly affected by their disadvantages. Although this is counter-intuitive, people want it to be true. This provides support for the "bootstraps" approach which places all the responsibility on the victim's ability to shrug off the influence of adversity. Even some of the women themselves claimed their stress never affected their achievement.

After exploring the definitions of resiliency, I found that some college professors make a distinction between invulnerability and resiliency. According to Rhodes and Brown (1991), the word "resiliency" most accurately describes those who have experienced dysfunctionality themselves and have bounced back after recovery. For example, an alcoholic who has been able to avoid alcohol might be placed under this category.

In Rhodes and Brown (1991) definition, the word "invulnerability" is used to describe those who have never allowed dysfunctional environments to affect their functioning. For a while I thought that I should call the women invulnerable. Those who were interviewed in this book have achieved highly since they were young children. Although some claimed they were precocious as children, some say they smoked pot as teenagers, and others experienced low self-esteem in high school, none of the women described a time in their lives when they had major problems "functioning."

I chose not to use the word "invulnerability" because I believe it is a myth that people are not affected by stress. I believe the women in this book were deeply affected by their misfortunes. When people face stress (such as a put-down from a parent or a teacher), they are hurt in some way, and then they may bounce back. If they are careful about protecting their image, it may seem as though they were never affected. For resiliency, image can be more important than reality. And what is reality in this situation? How can social scientists accurately measure how strongly a person is affected by pain and suffering? Social scientists compare the behavioral responses of individuals in an attempt to ascertain whether people respond in similar ways. Then they make assumptions that people who respond in the same way also feel the same. Unfortunately, there is no way for us to completely leave the isolation of our own bodies to understand other people's experiences.

The problems faced by the women in this book did affect their ability to achieve. Would they have achieved at a higher level if they had not faced the same stressors? Most likely, yes. But of course, without the influence of their backgrounds, these women would have been different people with different motivations. Therefore, there is no way to answer that question definitively. People who are resilient tend to find ways to turn disadvantage into advantage. Often their histories become part of their motivation to succeed. Several of the women in this book indicated that they spent time "proving" that people like "them" could make it. Others claimed that they were motivated to achieve because they didn't want their adult lives to be as bad as their lives as children.

Although I cannot claim that the women would have achieved at a higher level without their disadvantages, I can say with a great deal of confidence that without their barriers, they would have enjoyed the achievement process more. This is important because one of the reasons women from disadvantaged backgrounds may avoid higher education is that they fear the achievement process will be so unpleasant that ultimately the advantages of furthering their education will not outweigh the disadvantages. This is especially true because people from poor backgrounds are often skeptical that education will actually make their lives better. When I was young, I remember many times hearing stories about people who went to college and afterward could not find jobs. I never heard stories about people who went to college and did well.

PERSONALITY TRAITS AND ACHIEVEMENT

In this chapter, I describe and then connect a few common personality traits with the women's achievement process. It is important to understand the personalities of the women who were able to use education to their advantage. Often individual personality is ignored or underplayed because people like to place blame on family functioning. I found that personality and what I describe as personal response to environment were also important.

Independence and Maturity

All the women were mature and independent. Most had memories of being mature from a very young age because they had to grow up fast and accept responsibilities early. For example, many had to care for younger sibling and work as teenagers.

Donna: Obviously I was very self-sufficient. I was not a child at all. I managed all my own laundry, cooked all my own meals, did everything, at a very, very early age, so I was very self-sufficient.

Martha: When I was home, I was cleaning the house, I was cooking meals, I was taking care of my younger brother and sister. I don't remember having a lot of interaction with my parents during those years. They were just really unavailable because they had so much to deal with. They were very, very preoccupied with their own stuff.

Joy: I never did the high school giddy girlie stuff. I didn't go to my prom, and I think that I'm half jealous of those people who did and half scornful of them. I'm scornful because I'm jealous, maybe. I'm scornful, like I don't need that, because I didn't get it. And maybe I wish that I had got it, but I've always thought that all that giddy teenager stuff was beneath me, even when I was a giggly teenager.

Sara: I was always recognized as being much more mature than other children. Partly that was because I had already seen quite a lot at home that other children may not have seen, but I took that as an indication that I was superior to the other children.

Being independent did not always help them in school, however, because teachers do not always understand the needs of children who are mature in some ways and not in others. For example, these women had problems attracting mentors and getting high school counseling because teachers interpreted their maturity as a sign that they did not need help. This was exacerbated by the fact that as children, they never learned how to ask for assistance. They were afraid that if they asked for help (which was admitting vulnerability), they might destroy the impression of competence that they had worked so hard to create and maintain.

June: In a way there was a lot of separation between school and home, and in some ways that really worked for me. School was this secure place. I could be a different person at school than I was at home. I had the chance to be this highly functional person. Of course there were times when it would spill over; that was uncontrollable. Anytime I did have that spillover, when I couldn't keep my image together, I got negative reactions. And that was bad.

These women were not only afraid to admit lack of knowledge related to academic and career counseling; they were also afraid to admit it when they lacked basic skills. This does not mean that they graduated from school and could not read. All of them graduated from high school with outstanding, or at least above-average, grades and could pass achievement tests with average, if not above-average, scores. What I'm suggesting is that these women may not have reached their full potential because they were afraid of revealing any lack of knowledge. Some of this fear could have come from lack of knowledge about what is expected from a child at particular ages. They may have felt that because they were different, they had less knowledge than their privileged counterparts. This may have caused them to be afraid to reveal a lack of knowledge that they suspected was out of the ordinary.

It is possible that these children could have done more than some evaluation methods would indicate. Because they grew up fast, it seems that their thinking was quite sophisticated even while their knowledge in certain areas was incomplete. Many of them believed that they had something to offer but that no one recognized their abilities.

Debbie: I know so many women who have always wanted someone to say, "I can tell you're gifted, and I want you to stay in my class because you're really good in this particular area." I know so many women who have wanted that to happen. They all have this seed of awareness that they've got something really great to offer, they just don't know which direction to go. I never had that. I had a couple of people that I sort of poked at enough and they finally helped me work things out, that kind of thing.

The women were often judged as being below what they believed was their level of competence. Although they may have seemed extraordinary once it was understood where they came from, most people didn't have access to this information. So these women were judged according to criteria that were established for everyone from any background. Unfortunately, when they were evaluated in this way, they appeared average or slightly above average. The truth is that women in their circumstances do have potential that is often overlooked.

By the time these women became adults, their independent nature was so ingrained that they did not want help. Completing a task independently became more comfortable for them than asking for assistance. In graduate school, this caused the women to have difficulty attracting attention and seeking mentors.

Benevolence

The women in this book were well liked by their teachers. Many characterized themselves as the teacher's pet. From this description, readers may envision quiet and obedient young girls. This picture is not totally accurate. Each one had her own style. It is true that many were quiet, respectful, obedient and afraid to speak out. However, others were loud and boisterous and quick to call out an injustice. A few described themselves as precocious. In other words, the women did not all fit the stereotype of the sweet little girl who is afraid of her own shadow. However, that style was well represented. It is probably safe to say that these women were all nice girls, especially in elementary school. Even those girls who described themselves as precocious (which is a word many used when describing themselves as bad or rebellious) often took care of younger family members, were involved in Girl Scouts and earned straight A's in school. In high school, a small minority of the participants took drugs and were involved in other typical teenage troubles. One became pregnant at age 17. Others questioned authority and became part of the sixties movement to challenge traditional attitudes. These women occasionally described themselves as bad. Still, whether or not they were "bad," their antics seemed mostly to go unnoticed. It is safe to say that most of them maintained the reputation of being good girls, and although a few had some interesting experiences in their teenage years, most rode on a reputation that was established in earlier grades. None were incarcerated or expelled from school. None were labeled "bad" children and made to feel incompetent.

The fact that the women in this book were good girls is important. This personality trait is tied to the ability to attract attention and earn good grades in elementary school. According to Myra and David Sadker (1994), nice girls often rack up what they describe as apple-polishers' grades while lagging somewhat behind on achievement tests. This is directly tied to three findings from this project that are explored in detail later: (1) the importance of being recognized and reinforced in elementary school, (2) the disappointment later when being the good girl is no longer sufficient to attract attention and earn good grades, and (3) the ability to make teachers happy with appropriate behavior is often more important than learning information. If girls learn how to make people happy when they are young and if teachers are happy because a child is obedient (rather than questioning) or because she gets correct answers by memorization (rather than understanding the material), it is possible that students will strive to make teachers happy in whatever way is easiest. Besides, to young children, memorizing might represent the abstract concept of learning.

When the participants were young, most were good girls. As adults, they became caring women. Most of the participants had dedicated their lives to making the world a better place to live. For example, many were interested in education or psychology. Even those in business were interested in doing some work that would ultimately help the world. This could have been a characteristic of this particular group of women. Since these women were willing to be involved in this project, it is obvious that they were willing to expend energy to better society. However, this was a common personality trait that should be noted and valued.

Carmen: At that time my social consciousness kicked in and I really felt very, very strongly that I wanted to contribute to my community.
Pam: And you consider your community?

Carmen: The Chicano community. So what I consider success is, first of all, doing something that you love doing and that you're really committed to. For me personally, it's to make a difference in society, or to at least help in some way.

Joy: I want to close down every institution [for the disabled] in the entire United States. I've worked at five of them, and I feel I've been to hell—hades inner circle. I worked in an institute in Tunisia. I worked in the ugliest, baddest, most evil place on the face of the earth. There were 112 naked people behind bars. None of them had two ears. I wanted to fix them. I want to work myself right out of a job. I'm very passionate about the fact that it's nothing short of apartheid and it's cruelty. And I have seen some really horrific things that violate my sense of justice, and I want to stop that.

Self-Confidence

Many believe confidence is the key to success. Do these women have self-confidence? The answer is yes and no. A few of them claimed they were very self-confident and always had been since they were children. A few others said they lacked confidence and had suffered from low self-esteem since they were children. Most of the women, however, seemed to have a high opinion of their abilities in some instances and serious doubts about their abilities in others. They had the confidence that comes from success, but doubts still intruded upon their tranquillity. They battled self-esteem-damaging images from years ago, but to a lesser extent as they became older. As a global statement, these women probably have more confidence than many other women, if for no other reason than that they were able to muster enough confidence to try new things even when they faced the possibility of devastating rejections.

The quotes presented below illustrate how the women talked about themselves in contradictory ways. In most of the interviews, during one part of the discussion, they described their abilities in a way that would suggest they have confidence (even to the point of arrogance), and then later they described their fears in ways that would suggest they have been unconfident, even scared, at certain times during their educational process.

Confident

Jackie: I don't remember having to study in the lower grades. I've always read really quickly. Again, I don't want to sound like, oh, God, I'm so smart, but I've always read a lot and I've always read very quickly. I remember we had to take a speed-reading class, and I remember reading through these asinine little paragraphs, and since I could read through them well before the time allotted, I remember reading through multiple times and wherever I was when they rang the bell after having read it through several times, I'd tell them that's the line I was on just to keep it interesting.

Less Confident

Jackie: I thought, well, what the hell, I can apply for a doctorate and all they can do is tell me no. And I fully was expecting them to tell me no because I thought, What am I doing in graduate school? I did this on a lark, and they're taking it seriously.

A common theme presented in a recent book, *School Girls,* concludes that girls have more self-esteem when they are younger (in elementary school) and less as they get into high school (Orenstein, 1994). The women I interviewed often talked about their confidence in the lower grades and their fears in graduate school. Their lack of confidence was most often associated with the idea that they did not belong in graduate school. Some suggested that it was a mistake or a miracle that they were admitted to the schools they attended. Many described graduate school as overreaching. Psychologists have suggested that many people suffer from the "impostor complex" (Clance, 1985; Range, 1990), which is a psychological explanation for what happens when people feel that others around them are more capable. People who suffer with an impostor complex believe that if the truth about their abilities were known, they would suffer unfortunate consequences.

Most of the women in this book did suffer from the impostor complex. They felt they were different, especially in relation to their academic preparation, and they often attributed their achievement to luck.

Pam: Do you feel comfortable going and talking with professors?
Martha: I never did. It terrified me.
Pam: Why?
Martha: I always felt like they would just see a stupid person—that they would find out. I felt when I was in class, I wore a big mask and if they saw who the real me was, they would see through it all.

Did their attitude come from a lack of confidence? Were they insecure? Since these women experienced themselves as different, they seemed sensitive to suggestions that they were inferior. This kind of sensitivity is commonly attributed to irrationality, but these women were not irrational. Women from nontraditional backgrounds are constantly bombarded with messages telling them they are inferior. This often happens with minority women, who are accused of being in positions of power (e.g., academic positions, deanships) because of affirmative action rather than on the basis of their own abilities (Skinner & Richardson, 1988).

These women also lacked confidence when they were in a position to express a public voice. For example, Brandy was an architect, and she felt nervous whenever she had to present her designs to a group of people. Jackie felt nervous when she took her oral examination during her doctoral program.

Jackie: I had bad experiences, but it wasn't a function of anyone trying to make me feel that I didn't belong or that I wasn't any good. I think most of my stuff was internal, because throughout this process it was a struggle for me to feel like it was okay for me to be doing this. Like before I took my orals, for example, I mean, you know what fun that is. You know, happy, happy, joy, joy. When I was reading my stuff and writing my stuff and thinking my stuff, I was fine. But every time that I was in a position where they could finally say, the emperor really doesn't have any clothes, I would just be terrified. I don't remember my orals. I was so terrified. I had like sweat.

One last observation about confidence is that these women had difficulty understanding the balance between confidence and arrogance. Even when they talked to me, they felt the need to qualify or temper their comments about their abilities. They recognized the need to appear confident, and obviously in professional situations they have presented a confident image, but they did not seem to understand when they were being confident and when they were coming across as overreaching or arrogant.

Shirley: In my application to graduate school, I said I wanted to teach history and that I wanted to get a master's degree because I thought it was pretentious to suggest that I might want a Ph.D. So I didn't say I wanted to teach at the college level. The problem was that this Ph.D. program trains Ph.D.'s to become academicians, and I didn't know that. So I don't know if my application was ever seriously considered because of my goals statement. It's a misunderstanding of the process combined with self-esteem issues. Even if you secretly think you might be able to do it, you don't want to admit it to someone else because it sounds overreaching.

This may be a gender-related issue. In a related study, Daubman, Heatherington and Ahn (1992) found that women adopted a modest self-presentation style, which was motivated by the need to protect the self-esteem of the experimenter. So it is possible that women in general are modest and their modesty places them at a disadvantage when they're competing with men.

Another possible reason why women are confused about the difference between confidence and arrogance is that they are offended by arrogance and elitism in many school cultures. Modesty may be a reaction to their own feelings about morality. Also, the women in this book had a broad view of reality. In other words, it is possible that men do not always focus on what they don't know because they recognize this as counterproductive. In comparison, the women had a clear understanding of how much they did not know. Therefore, it was difficult for these women to feel that they were special, brilliant or important when so many other people around them were also special, brilliant and important. In sum, smart women may have a problem with confidence because (as has been comically portrayed in the media) they "think too much."

Perfectionism

The personality trait that was most commonly shared among the participants was perfectionism. They not only strove to be perfect as adults, they strove to be perfect as children.

Maria: Needing to learn English didn't bother me too much, but I do remember that after we moved to California (from Mexico), I remember getting my first report card. In the past, I had always gotten straight A's. There was no question. That time I think I got a C in spelling and a B in language, and I was so heartbroken. I worked really, really hard and by the end of that school year, I had straight A's again.

Some suggested, and it seems logical, that one reason they had to be perfect was to counter feelings of inadequacy. Some felt that being better than everyone else was a way to reassure themselves that they were equal.

Janus: Being smart made me feel equal; that's what it made me feel. It made me feel equal because I realized that our circumstances in my house were different from theirs. I mean much different, and so it made me feel equal. I don't know how; but it did, and maybe that was just me and how I dealt with it. But it made me feel like I was operating on even grounds here with these other kids.

In our society, many consider perfectionism a positive trait; however, for these women, perfectionism often affected the participants' experiences negatively. Their perfectionism was at odds with some of the basic structures in the school system. For example, one common method of instruction (whether good or bad) encourages students to try something new on their own. If they do it wrong, they are shown by experts how they can improve their performance. For perfectionists, this educational strategy is uncomfortable. Perfectionists want to be told how to do something right in the first place so that they receive nothing but positive reinforcement when they are done. Perfectionists do not like the style of teaching that focuses on what students do wrong. They do not like to be criticized, especially if they feel they did not have complete control over their performance in the first place. This happens when students are not adequately instructed on how to do a task correctly from the beginning. To perfectionists, being told how to do something better is not a learning experience, but a sign of failure.

Shirley: I have a very vivid recollection of being in first grade and we made hand prints in clay. We were supposed to take them home for our mothers. So I made my hand print in clay, and then afterward, the teacher criticized it because on the bottom there were all these cracks. Well, I didn't know how to avoid making cracks in the bottom of the thing, and nobody told me how I could avoid these cracks. I was trying to do a good job, so how could I have done it differently when nobody told me? At this point, I am very sensitive to being criticized for doing something, when there was no way I could have known to do it any differently. So when I feel like I'm being criticized for something that is not my fault, I get emotional.

Most of the women claimed that they depended on school for positive reinforcement. Perfectionists who depend on school for most of their reinforcement may be affected by the possibility of failure even more than other perfectionists. The result is that women such as those in this book become experts at learning "what the teachers want" rather than "what is important for them to know." Once again, this is an example of how these women's personalities clash with the traditional school structure.

Perfectionism can also be a negative if it affects a student's choice of classes and majors. This happened to some of the women in this book. For example, as the participants started making the transition into junior high and high school, many of them could no longer earn top grades in math and science, so they chose other classes that did not emphasize math. In these other subjects, they were, once again, the best. But unfortunately, they were never able to explore interesting careers in the areas they avoided.

Perseverance

To say that these women are persistent is stating the obvious. However, there are interesting observations associated with their perseverance that should be presented. These women expected an enormous amount of hard work and persistence from themselves. They rarely questioned the amount of energy they needed to expend to succeed. A few times I asked them if they were ever validated for their efforts. Most of them were confused by that question. In fact, many thought I was asking them if they had any friends. What I wanted to know was if anyone had ever acknowledged how hard they had to work to achieve at a level comparable to others who did not face similar barriers. In most cases, the women repeated what they had said earlier, which is that most people did not know where they had come from, so these people would not be in a position to validate their extra effort. After so many years of working under certain expectations with no validation, their extra hard work was considered normal. A few times when I asked if they were given financial support through school, some answered yes because they were able to get full-time jobs outside the university setting. For a while I thought they were misunderstanding my question until a few others asked me if I considered their "jobs" (again, outside the school setting) as financial aid. Working full-time and going to school was accepted by these women as a normal necessity. They did not consider this experience unusual.

Expectations are an important part of the achievement puzzle. Most of the women did not expect the schools or their families to provide for them. They believed that students had to fight to get the type of education they needed. In fact, women were quick to recognize dysfunction in their families and not so quick to recognize dysfunction in school settings. This is important because if a perfectionist believes that it is normal to struggle through school, she is more likely to bounce back after receiving criticism or experiencing failure. In this chapter, I discussed the fact that some of the women lacked confidence and blamed themselves for their failures. Still, they found ways to counteract feelings of inadequacy. Perhaps perseverance and the attitude that hard work and struggle are normal helped these women compensate for their insecurities. The idea that all students must struggle allowed them to maintain a higher sense of self-esteem in the face of criticism. They persisted because they recognized struggle as part of the process, not a sign of their inadequacy. Some perfectionists believe that if they have to struggle, it is because they are not smart enough or talented enough. For the women in this book, since struggle was a normal part of their lives outside of school, it was perceived as a normal part of their lives in school as well. They were ambivalent about their self-esteem because they recognized that some struggle is normal, but they wondered if others were dealing with the struggle better than they were. This may be one reason why women like to talk with each other (sometimes complain) about their progress. They need to confirm that others feel the same as they do in similar situations. This is a coping strategy. In other words, the women's persistence, combined with their belief that people need to struggle, helped them to counteract the low self-esteem associated with their histories.

SUMMARY AND DISCUSSION

Other researchers have identified and described the personality traits of children who are resilient. For example, Werner and Smith (1983) conducted longitudinal studies in Hawaii with children whom they categorized as vulnerable but invincible. In that study, they followed children who were exposed to biological risks at birth (low birth weight) and then raised in less than optimal environments.

Werner and Smith (1983) studied more than just final outcomes for these children. Their study included a two-year follow-up, a 10-year follow-up and an 18-year follow-up. Through the years, their research team observed behaviors, assessed environmental factors and interviewed significant others. They watched how these children interacted with people and how others responded to them. They followed their medical progress as well as their academic and professional development. Their research supports the conclusions that children who are resilient have these characteristics in common:

- An active, evocative approach toward solving life's problems, enabling them to negotiate successfully an abundance of emotionally hazardous experiences
- A tendency to perceive their experiences constructively, even if they caused pain or suffering
- The ability, from infancy on, to gain other people's positive attention
- A strong ability to use faith to maintain a positive vision of a meaningful life
- A tendency to be more active, more flexible and more adaptable even in infancy

Many of the women interviewed in this book shared some common characteristics. For example, they were independent and mature for their age, which made them more interested in an independent (adult) style of education. Unfortunately, it also caused educators and counselors to believe that they did not need help; so often they received inadequate counseling in high school and college.

Most of the women grew up as good girls (even those who described themselves as precocious which is a word some used when describing themselves as being bad) and later became women who cared about making the world a better place for themselves and for others. This is important because many girls act nice to gain the teacher's attention, which causes the teacher to respond positively to their behavior and pay less attention to their academic needs. This may help to explain why girls often do well in elementary school and do less well in high school.

The women in this book were ambivalent about their confidence. Sometimes they were confident to the point of arrogance, and at other times they were afraid to talk to professors because they did not feel worthy. Ultimately, they found enough confidence to try even when they faced rejection.

The women were also perfectionists. Although this trait helped them achieve at a high level, it also made the educational process more difficult because their style was at odds with instructional methods that focus on what students do wrong. The participants were dependent on getting positive feedback from school. Criticism was intolerable.

Finally, the women were persistent, but in a way that precluded them from recognizing the difference between the level of work they demanded of themselves and that required of other students. For example, many believed that working full-time during school was a normal way for students to support themselves through college. There was no recognition that many other students did not work full-time during their undergraduate experience. Ultimately, since they had to struggle in their personal lives, they accepted the need to struggle in school.

4

RELATIONSHIP WITH DISADVANTAGE

During my very first interview, I talked with Janus, an associate professor in a speech and hearing department. Within the first few minutes of the interview, she complained to me that she was frequently annoyed because her colleagues in the education department often approached her and described how disadvantaged children felt, what they needed and why they needed whatever they were suggesting. She continued by saying, "Did these people ever consider the possibility that they were talking about me? I was that disadvantaged child. I was that African-American girl who grew up in a poor urban neighborhood. I was that 17-year-old girl who became pregnant and then raised a child on my own while finishing high school and then college. I was that child, and they were telling me how I felt and what I needed. I found that offensive." I went on to ask her how she responded to these proclamations. Specifically, I asked her if she had ever revealed her personal experience with the topics they were discussing." She hesitated for a moment and then said, "No, and to be honest, I'm not sure why."

I understood how Janus felt. I remember once having a discussion with a colleague about a low-income housing project in a Black neighborhood. He explained to me how the children who lived there felt. He pointed out the overcrowding, the lack of air conditioning and the unkempt buildings. I listened and became more annoyed as he continued making assumptions that I had no idea what he was talking about. I finally said to him, "You know, this is actually quite familiar to me because, as a child, I lived in a few housing projects."

That was all I said. I never told him that I had experienced a five-person family living in a one-bedroom apartment. I never told him that I was often called the "project kid" and forbidden by parents to play with their children. I never told him that although I was white, I had lived in a number of low-income Black neighborhoods. Although I wanted to, I did not tell him that as a child I had also lived in an abandoned trailer and in a barn. I mentioned only that I had lived in a housing project. His response was silence. He never did acknowledge my comment. He never asked me another question about my background. In fact, after a few moments of silence, he continued his pedantic explanation of "their" plight and ignored my comment completely. Later I found that although this man was Black, he was raised by a wealthy family in England. He attended elite private schools, and as an adult, he had traveled the world. To this day, I have not discussed my past with this particular colleague, and he continues to believe that he is the expert on "those" children.

I am not alone in being reticent to discuss my disadvantage. Nor was I alone in having received strange responses when I did discuss it. Many of the women who volunteered for this project had an interesting relationship with disadvantage. In other words, the way they felt, responded and disclosed information about their history was an important part of their achievement process. In this chapter, I describe the women's relationship to disadvantage. Specifically, I talk about the way they define disadvantage and when and how they disclose information about their nontraditional backgrounds.

DEFINING DISADVANTAGE

Many of the women I interviewed questioned their status as disadvantaged. Often when a woman called to volunteer, she was quite concerned about whether she was truly qualified. This was an interesting contradiction, since most of the women had experienced serious difficulties as children, including poverty, sexual and physical abuse, mental illness, alcoholism, family discord, racism and sexism, and many other stressors. Still, some had difficulty categorizing themselves as disadvantaged. Other researchers have also found that people tend to deny personal disadvantage (Crosby et al., 1989). Crosby claimed it was easier for women to acknowledge that women in general were discriminated against, but many denied that they had personally experienced discrimination themselves.

Obviously, the word "disadvantage" had varied meanings to different people. In fact, each woman emphasized different aspects of her disadvantage. For example, some claimed they were disadvantaged as children because their families were poor. Others associated disadvantage with family functioning. Still others claimed to be disadvantaged because they had no guidance from their parents. I have taken the position in this book that these and other forms of stress and inequity represent different forms of disadvantage.

There are many reasons why the women may have been hesitant to adopt the label of disadvantage. First, disadvantage is often defined according to some type of imaginary scale. It is inevitable that someone else is more disadvantaged than you. It can seem pretentious to claim that you have faced adversity. And, the participants were extremely modest.

Also, some definitions of disadvantage are associated with functioning. In other words, some believe that a person can only be disadvantaged if the stress they endure negatively affects another part of their life. Schools often adopt this definition and label students "disadvantaged" if they do poorly in school.

Diane: My dad was an extreme alcoholic and a gambler. So that's what I grew up with for as long as I can remember. But I can't honestly say that was a disadvantage. I can't point to it and say, well, because of my dad, I've done poorly. I don't consider that a disadvantage in school at all. I can't honestly remember not turning in a homework or a paper because I was upset or up all night—which happened a lot. I never let it bother me that way.

Finally, since the word "disadvantage" has been considered racist, the women of color were most cautious about claiming they were disadvantaged. Yet they were less reticent to claim that they had been oppressed or discriminated against. In fact, none of the women who were ethnic minorities claimed to be disadvantaged because of their race However, all four agreed that they had experienced some type of discrimination because of their ethnicity. This is an interesting contradiction, since most would agree that discrimination puts people, especially children, at a disadvantage. Nonetheless, because of their personal feelings about the word "disadvantage," a few were uncomfortable describing themselves in that way.

The white women had different feelings. They were frustrated, believing that people were unwilling to acknowledge their disadvantages because they were white.

NEGATIVE CONNOTATIONS OF DISADVANTAGE

The women believed that being disadvantaged as children reflected on them negatively. In fact, very few participants felt comfortable talking about their background with anyone. Some were comfortable discussing these issues with friends, and some went as far as telling a professional colleague, but they disclosed information rarely. In fact, most women were quite steadfast in their belief that the reason they had been successful was because they had hidden their backgrounds.

Helen: I have never disclosed my background to anyone. Part of the reason I am successful is because I downplayed my background. In fact, it was disconcerting when I saw your message and I thought, ohh, I should have my say. Here's an opportunity for me to talk about this since I have never talked about this before to anyone. My background and my situation was an essential part of why I was not getting anywhere. So you have to get around that if you're going to get anywhere. One way that you can get around your background is to be like someone else. The way I do this is to not only mimic them in terms of their route, but also mimic them in the way that they are. So in a sense, I discard my past. I think it was necessary to let people believe things about me that were not true but were in keeping with where I had come to.

Pam: So people thought that you were middle-class?

Helen: They certainly thought I was middle-class. At least middle-class, and I let them believe that. They certainly thought that my family was college educated, had a little bit of money and so on, and I let them believe that.

Pam: And you think it would have gone against you if they had known?

Helen: Um-hum, I think it would have.

Pam: And you still think that's true today?

Helen: Yes, well, I don't know. I've thought about this. Has it changed any? I think at the time, I did it the right way. Now its different. In fact, your study wouldn't have happened 20 years ago. You wouldn't be here. I wouldn't be talking about this. Until I came to California no one invested in people like me. So I was not going to tell somebody that I was one of those people and then ask them to invest in me. Maybe it's changed for some people. There was a woman recently who was the graduate of the year who was talking about having come from a very disadvantaged family. She was doing this and being celebrated for it. I think there is that. On the other hand, she's Hispanic, and I think that we might be doing this for some people from ethnic groups, but I don't know if we're doing it for white people. I think it still might be the same for white people.

Jackie: I'm not going to be extraordinarily closeted about my life. But at the same time, if I'm presenting something, I want it to be on the validity of the data. Like for my thesis, I have 400 references. I don't want people to think they're getting the authentic experience, which is related to the authentic Black experience or the authentic female experience. I'm probably reacting too much, because if there's some question about Black people, then everybody will turn around and ask, "What do you think about that?" I'm not willing to speak for Black people. However, I also think that the way that white men transform their knowledge, their personal knowledge as well as their objectively derived knowledge, is taken for granted. And of course their personal experience is unfolded while they're doing their work, just as mine unfolded. But they're allowed to be intellectual about it. They're allowed to be professional about it. They're allowed to be "objective," in big quotes, about it. But when a woman, a person of color, or someone who's used drugs comes forth and says, well, this is what's going on—then it must be from personal experience because we are all little subjective feeling lumps. I want to be taken seriously.

Pretending to be someone else was quite simple. None mentioned the need to lie about their history. Since they were high achievers, people made incorrect assumptions about their backgrounds. Most of the participants simply never corrected friends' and colleagues' faulty assumptions. Although the participants did make some attempts to mimic people who were middle- or upper-class in style and appearance, they didn't have to try too hard. The images presented in the media about poverty and family dysfunction are often incorrect and sensationalized.

Martha: People often made assumptions about me, especially at the Hebrew University. Since I was a person coming to Israel from the United States, people thought I was wealthy, had supportive parents—who were good Jewish citizens—who cared about religion, which is all untrue. I just let it happen. I decided to allow them to think that way. I was never comfortable talking about who I really was. It was oppressive, but later on, I learned how to be more real and honest and incorporate that into my writing.

The women of color faced a more difficult time hiding their identity. Their skin color identified them as part of an oppressed group. Although the participants from ethnic minority groups could not completely hide who they were, faulty assumptions were also made about the women of color in this book. Since they were doing well in school, it was assumed that they did not face stress at home and therefore did not need as much counseling and support as other students. Also, although the women of color in this book could not completely fit into the mainstream, all claimed that they were comfortable in both the majority culture and their culture of origin. The importance of being comfortable in different cultures was supported in another project where Hispanic women were interviewed (Gandara, 1982). Gandara found that the participants were quite comfortable in both cultures and attributed part of their success to this comfort.

The women felt a need to hide their backgrounds because although difference was touted as being valued, they felt that people disliked and distrusted certain types of difference. Participants also mentioned that gender differences were not valued. Some participants felt that as long as they "thought like men," they were accepted and even treated well in school and at work.

Finally, since these women felt they had to hide who they were to succeed, I thought it was worth asking whether they themselves believed their disadvantages had detrimental effects on their personal and professional development. Many believed that although their backgrounds made the achievement process more difficult, ultimately their unique experiences helped them in their careers. Most claimed that their disadvantages made them stronger people, helped them to better understand others, gave them important insights about class and ethnicity, and motivated them to achieve. So ultimately, the women were hiding what they considered an important and positive part of themselves because they believed society considered it a negative attribute.

CONSEQUENCES OF FORCING STUDENTS TO HIDE THEIR IDENTITIES

As I mentioned earlier, many of the women questioned whether or not they were disadvantaged. As children, they had no idea that they were disadvantaged.

Furthermore, those who were ethnic minorities downplayed racial issues. The way that women define and experience disadvantage and race can be important, especially if they achieve at higher levels when they are not aware of or do not acknowledge their disadvantages. One goal of this project was to explain why some women can achieve despite stress, but another goal was to understand why only a few women from this particular population ultimately succeed. What are the consequences of forcing women to hide their backgrounds? Did this attitude allow them to achieve at the level they now enjoy? Or did this attitude drain their energy, making academic achievement a difficult challenge that only a few strong, resilient women were able to accomplish?

One consequence of hiding their backgrounds was that these women experienced themselves as being different. Whether or not others experienced them or perceived them as different, they considered themselves different. They made some of the same assumptions that others made about them, which is that they were surrounded by the middle class.

Joy: When I went to Harvard, the first three months I was walking around panicked, thinking, What am I doing here? I can't believe I'm here. I think the difference with Harvard for me was the name. I felt I had leaped some huge barrier. I was a them now.

Toni: This may sound like self-pity, but sometimes I feel illegitimate in some way.
Pam: Like you're not supposed to be there or something?
Toni: Right. Like I'm an impostor. It's just because everybody else is different? I feel like I didn't learn some social graces or something that they learned.

They felt they were deficient, especially in relation to their academic preparation, and they often attributed their achievement to luck. This has serious consequences for self-esteem, because none of the women experienced this difference as conducive to building self-esteem. On the contrary, many experienced the belief about their deficiency as being quite damaging to their self-esteem.

It is interesting to note that for the most part, the women considered themselves deficient for different reasons. Many believed they had an information deficit. In other words, they felt that other students knew more about "the system" than they did. Some believed they were not as academically prepared as others. In other cases, they felt they did not dress, talk or present themselves in as polished a manner as those from the privileged majority. If they associated too closely with negative functioning in their family, they may have experienced themselves as being less intelligent, more emotional, less articulate and less assertive. This caused many of them to feel that they did not belong in most of the educational institutions they attended. They felt that only students with certain backgrounds were really welcome.

When people from diverse backgrounds hide who they are to fit in, this gives an illusion that everyone is the same and competing on an equal basis. One participant said that all the other students in her program had parents who were professors. This may or may not be true, because others may also be hiding the truth about their backgrounds. Even when the participants recognized (on some level) that they had to face more barriers than other students, this realization was ignored, by them and by others. Ultimately the extra effort they made was invalidated.

It should also be mentioned that just as privileged people may not understand what it is like to be disadvantaged, those who face barriers do not always know what it means to be privileged. Although many women believed that everyone else was privileged, they did not seem to understand exactly what that meant. None acknowledged (at least on the surface) that some children grow up in supportive, loving families with parents who provide for their needs and pay their way through college. The women in this book believed that although everyone else was privileged, for some reason, these people still faced serious problems. In essence, many of them believed that everyone was privileged (which meant they were less equipped than other students) and at the same time, they believed that everyone faced problems (which meant they were not less equipped than other students). This characterizes a type of denial. These women believed they were different, but did not fully understand (or want to understand) the repercussions of that difference.

Another consequence of reinforcing the myth that everyone is the same and competing equally is that ultimately the women blamed themselves rather than the system for their failures. Other professionals in education have also found this to be true (Gandara, 1982: Kanoy, Wester & Latta, 1990). The women had extremely high standards for themselves and saw achievement as completely dependent on their own abilities, not on the school and not on their family. So, if they failed, it was a reflection on them, not on their parents or on an educational system that discourages achievement among certain populations. This attitude can be helpful if it encourages women to believe they have control over their lives and motivates them to take responsibility for improving performance. Interestingly, however, while the women were quite willing to take responsibility for their problems, they did not take credit for their successes. This observation has also been documented elsewhere (Gandara, 1982: Kanoy, Wester & Latta, 1990).

If these women take responsibility for their failures (with no regard for alternative explanations) and do not balance this responsibility by crediting themselves for their achievement, it is no wonder that the academic process is unpleasant for them. In addition, when women blame themselves for their difficulties, they often expend an enormous amount of energy to prove themselves. Once again, this can ultimately motivate students to do well, but it makes the process very tiresome.

SUMMARY AND DISCUSSION

Why do people have complicated relationships with disadvantage? Sometimes associating yourself with disadvantaged or minority groups and disclosing information is helpful, and sometimes it is detrimental; sometimes it is a sign of neurosis, while at other times it is a sign of mental health; sometimes it can help a student get into a graduate program, and sometimes it causes an individual to be rejected (Chase, 1990). Right now the social norms surrounding self-disclosure and stigma are changing, and people do not know how to respond to these changes. In fact, it is possible that the popularity of talk shows has been a direct result of the confusion surrounding changes in self-disclosure patterns. In some ways, talk shows exploit people's need to share their experiences, while they also exploit the fact that self-disclosure is still taboo. In other words, people are a little shocked at the disclosure they witness on talk shows, yet they are curious to hear people's stories; this ultimately bolsters ratings, but it does not provide an appropriate outlet for open communication.

Why is it important to discuss women's relationship to personal disadvantage? One implication of hiding the truth is that adults are not the only people affected by our social norms and expectations; children are also affected (Saarni, 1979). If adults hide their histories to adapt to social norms, it is inevitable that children will also hide who they are. Children might not understand the complex pressures associated with their behavior, but children quickly pick up cues on how to behave. At this time it is also possible that children do not tell others about their situations because, as a society, we have set up a system where disclosure can have more serious consequences than the dysfunction children face at home. The women in this book believed that hiding their families' situations helped them to succeed as adults and as children. They were probably correct. It is almost certain that many adults do not know how to handle uncomfortable family-related problems. If adults are hesitant and incompetent when dealing with family problems, they could ultimately make the situation worse for children who face stress. Children who sense hesitation will not understand that adults simply do not know how to handle the situation; they will interpret adult hesitation to mean that they don't deserve help or don't really need help. Children might also sense that once they disclose personal information, judgments will be made about who they are which could cause teachers to lower their expectations. Research has demonstrated the negative effects of teachers' low expectations on a child's educational achievement (Jussim, 1993). In addition, our system of assistance can have a negative effect on more than just teachers' expectations. It was interesting that as children, none of the women in this study dealt extensively with our system of assistance. None were placed in foster homes, drug rehabilitation facilities or juvenile detention facilities. In other words, these women had problems at home, but they were not exacerbated by the problems they could have faced in the system.

It was quite clear that these women did not trust the schools to provide helpful interventions.

Pam: Did you ever tell the school about your problems?
Jackie: Of course not! Why would I want them to know? Maybe I'm "of coursing" you too much, but I can't understand why I would want them to know that I'm an absolute wreck. That seems a little self-defeating. Everybody is patting you on the back because you're doing well in school. I was getting all the positive strokes for not being a suicidal maniac. Why change that? Things were good. Things were okay the way they were.

Another consequence of hiding personal history is that it precludes children and adults from connecting their learning with personal experience. Some investigators, especially in adult education, emphasize the need for women and nontraditional students to connect new knowledge with personal experience (Bartolomé, 1994; Clinchy, Belenky, Goldberger & Tarule, 1985; Terenzini et al., 1993). At this time, it is still difficult for women to relate their learning to positive personal experience, let alone negative experience. For example, in her article, Tarule (1988) outlines the problems associated with women bringing their experiences into the learning process.

In classroom discussions, women often join the dialog starting with long stories that detail what seems relevant from their lives. They ground their learning and understanding in their experience, while the listeners, students and instructors alike, squirm, unable to hear the logic of connection, and therefore the essence of the idea. The listeners are simply mortified by an apparently inappropriate sharing of life experience. They roll their eyes, the instructor tries to figure out how to break in, and the speaker begins to perceive that her presentation of the ideas, as well as the way she thinks about them are wrong (Tarule, 1988, p. 26).

Bringing personal experience into the learning process is difficult for everyone, but it is even more so for women from disadvantaged backgrounds. Even those educators who advocate a connection between learning and personal experience often inadvertently send subtle messages about what experiences are acceptable. This is a outgrowth of the trauma inflicted upon ethnic minorities as a result of the deficit model. Because of this injustice, teachers have had to fight negative stereotypes that present ethnic parents as dysfunctional and their children as deficient. Therefore, many do not want to hear about negative experiences that might feed into damaging stereotypes.

An example of a well-intentioned teacher subtly suggesting what is appropriate for people from disadvantaged backgrounds to discuss openly can be identified in a recent article by Bartolomé (1994). In her article, Bartolomé describes problems associated with the deficit model. She believes that a child's past should be incorporated into the learning process and that teachers should value what these students bring to the classroom. Unfortunately, as she presents this important message, Bartolomé is also subtly communicating which experiences are acceptable and which are not. In her article, Bartolomé gives an example of a teacher who was prejudiced against Hispanic children. After the teacher spent a semester getting to know a Hispanic child, she discovered his "loving and sunny" personality, which changed her attitudes toward Hispanic children. Bartolomé provides an example of the student's writing that turned his teacher's negative attitudes around. In that essay, the student praises his father for the hard work he has done and explains how his father has pulled the family out of poverty by sheer determination. If this was the child's experience, that is wonderful; however, what if the student had written a well-thought-out description of how his father's abuse had changed his life by inspiring him to become a lawyer and fight for children's rights? The question is, after reading this slightly different version, would the prejudiced teacher still think of the student as loving and sunny? Probably not!

Many are still not willing to accept students who are different. They are obsessed with trying to prove that we are all the same, and that "the same" means perfect. What Bartolomé is suggesting from her example is that once a teacher learns the truth about "these" children, his or her ugly stereotypes will drift away and the teacher will recognize that all parents are perfect and that problems only really exist in the stereotyped image of minority children. Pretending to be perfect is what the white population has done in the past. In fact, the white majority has worked hard to project a "we don't do that kind of thing" image. It should be emphasized, however, that some would claim that for Caucasians, this attitude grew out of ethnocentricity, and for ethnic minority populations, it grew out of a need to convince Caucasians that ethnic families were not all dysfunctional.

Bartolomé says that we need to value and use what students bring to their educational experience; this is true, but we must value not only soft, fuzzy experiences that convince others that deep down we are all angelic, but also our negative experiences. Our negative as well as our positive experiences make us all part of the human race and truly similar. By pretending that dysfunction doesn't really exist, we may be protecting parents and convincing outside observers that certain groups are not as bad as they have been portrayed in offensive, prejudiced descriptions, but we are also invalidating the experiences of children who face stress.

5

TEACHERS

It is common for people to remember and idolize a special teacher. Every woman in this book could tell a story about a special teacher who made a difference in her life. This teacher was usually someone who made a special effort to help her, in ways that defied conventions. For example, Donna was particularly grateful to a principal in her elementary school who snuck into her files and changed all of her low grades to straight A's. Since the principal knew that Donna was being physically abused by her mother, she changed all her grades and gave her a glowing recommendation so that Donna would be accepted into a private boarding school. In that school, Donna earned straight A's and later did exceptionally well in college and graduate school.

Maria told a story about how her sixth-grade teacher changed her life when he questioned the standardized predictions of her success. In her elementary school, children were given placement tests in the third grade. At that time, Maria had recently moved from Mexico and was still struggling to learn English, so she did poorly on her placement test. Her sixth-grade teacher asked her to retake the test after being convinced that she was achieving beyond predicted levels. The second time around, Maria scored high enough to be placed in the gifted math classes at her junior high school. After that, her reputation and her feelings about herself changed completely.

TEACHING STYLES

For most if not all of the women, a teacher's personality was more important than his or her teaching style. Although most of the women had a preference for a certain teaching style, they quickly adapted to various teaching strategies. Interestingly, but perhaps not surprisingly, there was no particular style that was generally best for everyone. Some liked lectures; some liked cooperative learning groups; some enjoyed independent study. The women's ability to adapt to different teaching styles may be a trait found more often among high achievers. Some of the women themselves commented that children who do poorly in school may be more affected by different teaching styles.

Janus: I think I can learn from any professor. I adapt to different teaching styles. I think we learn to do that along the way. Certainly some teachers are better presenters of the information than others, but I adapted to a lot of different teaching techniques and styles and they never bothered me. I just assumed, well, this is the person's style, so let me adjust.

Janet: I believe that anybody who wants the education can get it wherever. Certainly, I've seen differences in quality of education. I've taught at four different universities, so I see the quality differences, but I still think it is incumbent upon the student. If they want to be a good student, they can be a good student in any environment. It's really the rare, pitiful educator who can stand in the way of a good student doing well. Only if they actually demotivate the class could they accomplish that task. I think a good student will thrive in any environment, and it's the ones who aren't good students that really require the extra teaching effort. That's my belief.

The only consensus on teaching was that the women wanted a challenging curriculum. Often they were bored. This is not surprising. Not only is it intuitively obvious, but other investigators who have studied the needs of disadvantaged children (mainly referring to low achievers) have found that many preferred a speeded-up rather than a slowed-down curriculum. Levin's (1987) Accelerated Schools Program and Slavin and Madden's (1989) Success for All Project have clearly demonstrated that engaging students in a challenging, speeded-up as opposed to a slowed-down curriculum has positive academic and social outcomes. This also supports the dismal outcomes of children who are labeled slow learners and tracked into low-ability classes (Oakes, 1985). Rutter (1979) suggested that children benefit from attending schools not only that set high standards, but also those where teachers provide good models of behavior, where children are praised and given responsibility, and where conditions are safe and pleasant. Since these investigators were most often describing the needs of children who do poorly in school, it follows that students who do well, despite difficulties, would also want a challenging curriculum.

Janet: I don't know if I felt the esteem impact of being tracked high, but I definitely allied to learning at a pace that was more challenging. We got more interesting projects in science, and I felt a little more like I was stepping up to the plate and actually using my noggin.

Carmen: I remember one teacher in high school who was just really, really, really tough, and everybody was having such a hard time in her class. But on the other hand, she really made us work, and she had really high expectations. And even though you complain about it and you think it's unfair at the time, those are the professors that I learned the most from, because they really expect so much from everyone. It makes me expect more from myself.

Pam: Why was this junior high school so good?
Joy: They had high expectations. There wasn't a standard. There wasn't a you-have-to-do-this-and-then-you're-done attitude. There was no end in sight at the ashram. You just worked as hard as you could until the school year was over; your summer break was your end.

Shirley: Part of my rebellion in high school was because of the total lack of challenge in the school. The principal acknowledged that at one point where he was telling me that he had no intention of changing the curriculum to suit one student—the curriculum was geared toward the majority of students, and that it worked fine for them, and that if I happened to have needs that were different—tough luck. I remember at the time it confused me, because he was telling me that I wasn't going to get something that I didn't remember ever asking for, although I think they should have been providing it.

Teresa: The biggest contrast for me as a kid was going from what was done in America to what I faced in the Jesuit schools overseas.
Pam: How was that different?
Teresa: Challenging. You had to write all the time, you had to defend everything. You had to cite your sources. You were expected to be a scholar. You didn't go to school, you were a scholar. I mean it's a whole different orientation.

Ultimately, teaching style was not as important to the women as the way they were treated by their teachers. This may be important, since Hearn and Olzark (1981) found that women chose majors according to perceived level of departmental caring. In their study, Hearn and Olzark found that men tended to opt for unsupportive departments and majors that provided high-status rewards, whereas women exhibited the opposite pattern.

What did the women want from teachers? They wanted teachers to care about them as individuals. They wanted recognition, and they preferred a teacher who was nontraditional. The reason they were interested in nontraditional professors is that the teachers served as role models. Since the women defined themselves as nontraditional, they were encouraged by teachers who were also nontraditional.

Joy: One of the teachers spoke at our freshman orientation to welcome incoming students and parents. He said, "You brought your children here and you've entrusted them to higher education, and now they're just like you. If they could vote tomorrow, they'd vote for the same president, they'd use the same soap and they'd buy the same kind of paper towels you do. And I'm going to take your little tubs of shit and show them the world." He was drunk, and people were horrified. And he got reprimanded. But I was like, cool, I'll take his class. That was actually a great class, too. So what stands out for me are the radicals, the people who weren't behaving as they were supposed to, but somehow held up in this system. Their nontraditional behavior was somehow excused because their students were learning and they were doing good. And that's who I thought I was going to be.

After listening to what these women say they needed from teachers, it is possible to hear some familiar ideas that are embedded in different types of progressive pedagogies such as multicultural pedagogy, feminist pedagogy, critical pedagogy and constructivist pedagogy (Riviera & Poplin, 1995). For example, the women emphasized their relationships with their teachers which is an important idea embedded in feminist ideology. The women also embraced high academic standards which encourages children to be scholars and develop critical thinking. This is an important aspect of each of the different pedagogies listed. Still, the women quickly adapted to different teaching styles and never questioned how they were taught. In fact, very few commented specifically on the pedagogical methods they were exposed to in school and what did or did not work for them. Some professionals would attribute this to the way students are taught to passively accept the voice of authority (Freire, 1970). Freire would argue that students should be actively involved in their learning process.

RECOGNITION OF BEING SMART OR SPECIAL

The women I interviewed wanted attention from their teachers, but not just indiscriminate attention; they wanted the teachers to recognize their special talents. These women received some type of positive reinforcement for their abilities all the way through school, but especially in the lower grades. As adults, most complained that they did not get enough reinforcement; however, they never gave up the idea that they had something special to offer. Early positive experiences carried them through when they had doubts about their abilities as adults.

Tina: I think I liked grade school because I liked the concept of getting good grades. All of a sudden I was getting some strokes for something, and I liked that.

Diane: I think that I always thought that I was smart. I would not come close to classifying myself that way now. But every time we had a get-together with the grandparents and my aunts and uncles, my parents would always say things about my being smart. And I think that I just came to believe that I was. Plus, I always got A's in my classes, and I was always, always the teacher's pet. And I'm the one who always had the right answer. Maybe it was because I got more attention from them.

Carmen: I think part of the reason I did well was because I went to kindergarten and first grade in the Barrio school and then I was bused to the other side of town to the white school. I can't say for sure how I would have turned out had I stayed in the original school, but I think that going to this other school might have benefited me. Because immediately when I got there, they started testing me for these special programs—gifted programs, and I don't know that they would have done that at the other school.

Martha: I have a lot of memories of being teacher's pet in a lot of different classes. In second grade, I remember one assignment where we wrote a story and made a book, and I remember writing a story and the teacher took me around to all the different second-grade classes and asked me to read it. I remember my impression was that when I was writing stories, I could do no wrong.

Ultimately, there were so many comments about recognition for being smart and special that I organized them according to different grade levels. This uncovered a pattern of reinforcement that was provided from elementary through graduate school. Inevitably, students received more positive reinforcement both in elementary school and in graduate school. In high school and in college women received less reinforcement. I also found that women did not do as well academically in high school and in college, and they did not feel as good about their experiences. The women needed to be told that they were smart and special to counteract negative feelings associated with being different.

Sara: Again in graduate school, it's like I'm the star student. I have a couple of professors who believe that clearly that I am a good student, and it's great because they ask me to be their teaching and be research assistants and stuff.

WOMEN PROFESSORS IN COLLEGE AND GRADUATE SCHOOL

As a response to inequity, colleges are attempting to attract a more diverse faculty. During the interviews, I asked the women whether they wanted or needed more women teachers. The answer was yes, which was not surprising. However, this answer is not as simple as it may sound initially. Although participants thought that it would be helpful to have more women teachers, primarily, this was because women served as role models. When female students saw women thriving in important positions in prestigious universities, they realized that it was possible for them to succeed at high levels. This was especially true for women of color, who appreciated seeing other women of color in positions of power.

Janus: That's when I knew that I wanted to get a Ph.D., because I was encouraged by so many women and there were African-American females around who were Ph.D.'s and I just admired them so much, and respected them so much. I still do to this day.

Maria: I interviewed for a scholarship right before I started Berkeley, and it was from the Alumni Association, but it was also from the Latino or Chicano Group from the Alumni Association, and so out of the two people that interviewed me, one of them was a professor on campus. It was like, my God, there are people that can do this who are Latino.

The reason this concept is not as simple as it seems is that, although women wanted role models, they wanted role models who were like them. Surprisingly enough, women are not all the same. For example, some girls may be encouraged by women who are strong political feminists and assertively speak out against injustice. Others might relate better to a cultural feminist who advocates valuing what has been described stereotypically as feminine. This was also emphasized by Edwards, Edwards, Daines and Reed (1984), who described the characteristics and behaviors of effective role models for Native American women. They emphasized the need for role models to understand Native American culture and to be aware of their own identification with what they described as "Indianess." People are not the same. It was clear that many of the women did not believe that the women in positions of power were "like them." Most believed that highly successful women were those who came from privileged backgrounds and acted like men.

Shirley: People now think the only issue is ethnicity, and I still think that economic level is an important issue regardless of ethnicity, and I think a lot of the things that people are attributing to ethnicity are actually economic. Economics doesn't explain everything, but it explains a lot. I'm reading that book right now, *Blacks at Harvard,* and one of the things that's clear is that some of the people who are writing essays about their experiences at Harvard come from families where their parents and the parents before them all went to elite Ivy League colleges.

The women also mentioned their disappointment in female professors because although these women were role models, they were not as supportive as was expected. Many of the participants felt more supported by men than by women. A few suggested that female professors acted like men (e.g., were competitive and ambitious) to compete successfully in an educational system developed by and for men.

Pam: In school, were you more afraid of men than women?
Martha: I think I was equally afraid of both. When I look back at the women professors I had, it seems to me that they worked hard to get where they were and they had this very authoritarian presence, very harsh presence. That scared me. It was like, you get with the program.

Therefore, these women believed that the only way to succeed was to think and act like men. Also, some felt that female teachers were threatened by or jealous of other female colleagues or even female students. Those who mentioned this did not report the same type of competition and jealousy from male professors.

Shirley: I'm not sure the problem would be solved by more women teachers. If you demonstrate competence to male teachers, they change their minds; and they deal with the product that you present. With women, the better you are, the worse it is, and the more funny they get about it.

Jackie: My analysis of what happened to this one female professor is that her graduate experience was immensely damaging. And she's a Black woman, and from what I gathered was treated in an immensely racist and sexist way, and she found it very damaging. And so I think that whatever kind of unprocessed pain she experienced is oozing out and hitting unsuspecting grad students. Other students in my department have had similar experiences with her.

There are reasons why women teachers may not seem supportive. First, since there are fewer women in academia, students are more likely to have male professors. Therefore, there is greater likelihood that a student will find a positive role model among the majority of people, who happen to be men. Second, women professors tend to be younger and in lower positions. Many are still trying to earn tenure and to prove themselves. In academia today, this is a difficult process that takes an exorbitant amount of time. It is conceivable that the majority of women teachers do not have time for their students. Finally some students may be more disappointed in women teachers because they have higher expectations for females. Some female professors have complained that they are expected to treat students better than men do (Basow & Silberg,1987; Caplan, 1994). Although this is truly a compliment, most women professors do not see it as a compliment. They believe it is sexist that students expect more from them than they do from men. Obviously, men and women should treat students equally well. Whether teachers should be approachable and caring is debatable. However, according to the women in this book, if educators want women from disadvantaged backgrounds to reach their full potential, teachers do need to be caring and approachable.

SUMMARY AND DISCUSSION

After I finished the interviews, it was possible to see what the women needed from teachers. First, teachers' personalities were more important than their teaching style. The women claimed they could easily adapt to different styles, but it was important for them to have teachers who were caring and attentive. Participants were also interested in teachers who were somehow different. They connected with radical teachers who were willing to be nontraditional in their teaching style.

The women also mentioned their disappointment in female professors. Although these professors were role models, they were not as supportive as was expected. Many of the participants felt that female professors acted like men to compete successfully in today's world. Also, the participants not only wanted women as teachers, they wanted women who were like them. For example, they wanted to see women of color and women from disadvantaged backgrounds in positions of power. Many thought that women who had achieved highly were all Caucasian women who had come from privileged backgrounds. Ultimately, though again not surprisingly, obvious characteristics like gender and ethnicity, while important, do not begin to address the whole story. A teacher who is approachable, supportive and, most important who understands and appreciates his or her students' experiences and contributions is probably what disadvantaged students need most. So much the better if the teacher is also a good role model because of gender, ethnicity and class.

6

MENTORS

In a recent book about how the poor get to college, Levine and Nidiffer (1996) suggest that whether or not poor kids go to college is significantly affected by whether or not they have mentors. This is an interesting conclusion, given that 17 of the 21 women interviewed for this book claimed they never had a mentor. The disparity in our findings could suggest differences in the groups that we interviewed. I focused on women who had stressful lives as children, who achieved highly throughout school and who ultimately earned graduate degrees. Levine and Nidiffer interviewed 24 people, both men and women, who were all undergraduate college students. Half of each group of men and women were attending junior college, and half were attending prestigious universities. My group was much less diverse.

I found that the women in this book were extremely independent and reluctant to ask for help. Although many educators stress the importance of mentoring, few consider how people initiate and form mentor relationships. According to Summers-Ewing (1994), potential mentors usually rely on the protégé not only to initiate the relationship but also to continue its existence. Therefore it is important to understand why some potential protégés will initiate interaction and some will not. In one of her comments, Shirley summed up the problems many of the women in this book experienced when seeking guidance:

Shirley: I think this business of mentorship, I think you have to be receptive and seek someone out, and I didn't do that, and that's one of the things I learned how to do later. I think there might be problems with people who have experienced trauma to the extent that they can't reach out to other people. They're really handicapped in the mentorship area. People reach out, but you reject them. You don't see as opportunities, things that are opportunities.

Turban and Dougherty (1994) found that protégés who were more likely to initiate mentoring relationships had an internal locus of control, high self-monitoring, high emotional stability and low negative affectivity. In addition, Fagenson (1992) found that protégés who initiate mentor relationships generally had a greater need for achievement and power than did nonprotégés. Also, women seek mentors less often than men (Martin, Harrison & Dinitto, 1983).

Although protégés usually seek out mentors, in some cases, mentors do initiate contact with their protégés. According to Schappell (1990) and Scandura (1992), many mentors are attracted to protégés based on similarities in demographics, including gender, ethnicity, education, socioeconomic status and age. In fact, Scandura (1992) found that protégés who were most similar to their mentors, in terms of socioeconomic, educational and cultural backgrounds, received the best mentoring because they usually had higher-level mentors, and those mentors included them in after-hours socializing. Schappell (1990) also found that mentors were attracted to protégés who had the most promise of potential success in the organization. In other words, mentors were interested in finding protégés who ultimately would make them "look good" to the organization or to the university. Finally, Schappell also claimed that mentors sought protégés who were malleable. They wanted protégés who would be most affected by their counsel.

What I'm trying to point out is that people do not have an equal opportunity to benefit from mentors. Usually protégés are responsible for initiating mentoring relationships, and only those who have certain types of personalities are likely to initiate this type of contact. When mentors do seek protégés, they often choose protégés based on demographic similarities, potential for fame and malleability. Since nontraditional students are often shy about seeking mentors and since they did not have the same backgrounds as many of their potential mentors, they are at a disadvantage when seeking support. Although it contradicts some theories about how the poor get to college, I was not surprised that many of the women in this book never had mentors.

AVAILABILITY AND QUALITY OF COUNSELING IN HIGH SCHOOL

The women in this book started experiencing problems with guidance in high school. Since they did very well academically, most people would expect that they would receive information about college. Actually, I was shocked by the lack of guidance they received. And most of them were angry at the lack of academic guidance available to them in their high schools. Some were given no counseling; others received very little.

Carmen: I can't even remember ever meeting with a counselor. I don't remember any teacher or counselor ever telling me, "This is what you need to do." So I often wonder if it would have been better for me to apply to other colleges. Every college I've ever been to, I've only applied to one college and that's where I've gone every time. So I wonder if I had encouragement, would I have applied to more colleges and gone to better schools?

Tina: I think the reason I had no counseling was because I was poor and I was female. I had a 3.8 GPA. I had really high-any kind of test scores that you care to name, and yet nobody ever said the word "college" to me.

Brandy: I didn't really have support at home, and so I was on my own. I was choosing the classes I would take and deciding whether or not to go to college. I didn't really have any guidance, and I felt like I was floating. I didn't have guidance from either my parents or from people who were supposed to be like guidance counselors. There was never any kind of interaction with anybody who was really helpful.

In many similar situations, an author would point an accusing finger at school counselors. While counselors cannot be completely absolved of their responsibilities, after examining these women's stories in more detail, I have come to the conclusion that there were complex reasons why they may have been overlooked in high school. For example, it is possible that many were ignored because they worked hard to project the image that they did not need help. They had a very independent style, and they worked hard to hide their backgrounds. As was mentioned in previous chapters, these women were always mature and independent. Most have memories of being mature from a very young age because they had to grow up fast and accept responsibilities early. For example, many had to care for younger siblings and work as teenagers.

Being independent did not always help these women in school, because teachers do not necessarily understand the needs of children who are mature in some ways and not in others. As I mentioned earlier, these women had problems attracting mentors and getting high school counseling because teachers and counselors made the assumption that they did not need help. This was exacerbated by the fact that as children, these women never learned how to seek assistance, and they were often afraid to ask for help. They were afraid that if they asked for help they might destroy the impression of competence that they had worked so hard to develop and maintain. By the time these women became adults in college, their independent nature was so ingrained that they did not need or want help. Completing a task independently became more comfortable than asking for assistance.

Even those students who did receive some counseling in high school often described their experiences in a similar way. The counselor would ask them if they were going to college. Those who did plan to go to college would say, "Yes, I plan to go to University X because my friends are going there," or, "I've decided to go to College Y because that is the only school my family can afford." The most common response from the counselors was, "Okay," and then the counselors would send them on their way.

Shirley: Now that I know something about education, I went back and looked at my records, and it shocked me the lack of help and guidance that I received. I was a national merit finalist, which is a big deal. I had a four-year scholarship from the State of California. I could have gone to any school in the state of California—private or public. When I talked to my high school counselor, she spent all her time talking about my sister. She said, "Are you going to college?" And I said, "Yeah." And she said, "Where are you going?" And I said, "Well, I think I'll go to X College because a friend of mine is going there." She said, "Okay." Then we spent the rest of the time talking about my sister. Not because I brought it up, but because she brought it up.

Jennifer claimed she had a similarly nonproductive conversation with her counselor in high school. After studying her transcripts, I was not surprised. Jennifer was a straight-A student who had taken honors courses. She was involved in sports, the newspaper and student government. She had gone by herself to take a standardized test for admission into college. If I were her counselor, I would have considered seeking advice from her.

As part of their efforts to hide their backgrounds, the participants became experts at pretending they were knowledgeable and in control when in reality they were not. In many situations, they were afraid to ask questions because they thought their ignorance might betray their family situations. It was safer for them to continue learning on their own than to risk jeopardizing their reputations.

Also, they did not know how to ask for help and didn't realize what type of help was available. They learned to get information by reading people rather than by asking questions. When one of the women stated that she was going to College X because her family could only afford an inexpensive community college, this was not a statement, this was an indirect question. Her strategy was to wait for the counselor's reaction to determine whether she had any alternatives. In this way, she was able to reveal just enough about her situation without presenting details about her family life. When the counselor replied "okay," she had her answer. The message was received; for a student in her position, this was the best she could hope for.

Now these women look back and realize they had other options. They are angry because they wanted counselors to read their minds and magically understand what they needed without probing about their family life. Ultimately, they felt they were ignored for doing well and punished for staying out of trouble.

Janet: I'm interjecting my own theories here, but I believe you can't really judge a book by its cover. I wasn't a vocal student. I wasn't somebody who acted out. I wasn't somebody who was high throughout class and needed a lot of attention. It was only when people took the time to talk to me and acknowledge who I was—then they put things together and understood what I needed.

June: If I had been more like my brother, who caused trouble, then of course, schools respond to the troubled kids, the ones who are making noise. But when a kid's doing everything right, they don't notice. They're just grateful for having a good kid who doesn't give any trouble. My good behavior was reinforced and appreciated in that way, but nobody tried to understand what was really going on with this kid. I was very shy and withdrawn, but I think there were signals out there that I had problems. I don't think they were noticed because they weren't being looked for.

ABILITY TO SEEK MENTORS IN COLLEGE AND GRADUATE SCHOOL

It was not only in high school that many of the women were unable to seek help effectively. They also had difficulties attracting mentors in college and graduate school. Once again, those few who had mentors were aware of the importance of that assistance; the others were angry that mentors were not available.

Pam: Does your doctoral advisor know you as a person?
Toni: No.
Pam: Does he like you?
Toni: I think he likes me. I think he does.
Pam: Does he value what you have to offer?
Toni: I don't think he knows what I have to offer. He's really uninvolved with what goes on in the lab. He really doesn't know what I'm doing. He has never really known what I was doing.
Pam: How long have you been in graduate school?
Toni: Eight years.

Helen: I had no mentor. Did I later on have an informal mentor? Not really.

Jackie: The only time I talked to my advisor as an undergrad was when I decided to declare a double major, and literally our interaction was this: I had the forms. I said, "I want to do this." He said, "Do you think you can handle it?" I said, "Yes." He signed. That was it. That was all the advising I got during my undergraduate career.

Joy: Never. I've never had an advisor. Professor X will be my first advisor, if he actually is my advisor. I got all the way through the educational system without ever having an advisor.

Although many professionals continue to emphasize the importance of good mentors, as I mentioned earlier, few attempt to explain why some women easily attract mentors and others do not. Only a few in this book had good mentors who assisted them throughout their graduate education. And those who did usually did not independently seek out and attract their mentors. Instead, those who had mentors were usually placed together with certain professors through special circumstances, such as a class, a job, or a project. This provided the opportunity for the professors to get to know them and to care about them.

Michelle: I think my connections with teachers just happened. I never went to find a good advisor. I'm not that assertive that I seek people out. But it happened because they were people I had to work with. Like my thesis advisor; I had to go see him a certain number of times, and I had him as a teacher for several courses. Also, it was a small department, so we had a lot of one-on-one.

Janet: In graduate school, I started to work for the marketing department chairman, and about the time I was ready to graduate I asked him, "How come you hired me?" He had so many people he could have hired. And he said, "Well, because I saw your admissions test scores. They were about the highest of anybody that we admitted that semester." And also, he pulled some test scores from classes that I was taking my first semester and I was at the top. He said basically I was the top student in everybody's class. I didn't realize he was so behind the scenes, picking through my paper trail of tests and history to figure out who he should hire as a graduate student. So then basically, word of mouth after that. After you are established as somebody who works hard and is committed, I had professors ask if I would work for them.

One reason that many of the women had difficulties seeking out and attracting mentors in college was that they were intimidated by authorityand felt uncomfortable engaging professors on a one-to-one basis. Usually, they were afraid they would come across as ignorant, or they were afraid that what they had to say wasn't important. In other cases, they felt unworthy to take a professor's time because they believed the professor's time was too valuable to waste on them. Psychologists might attribute this to what they call the impostor phenomenon which describes an irrational fear in people that if others learn the truth about what they "really know" and how smart they "really are," they would be disappointed with the reality. The women in this book overwhelmingly suffered from this complex.

Brandy: I'm scared of seeking out professors for help. But I do think that they're there, and if I really wanted to go find them and nail them down and pester them, they would be there.
Pam: Why? Are you afraid of them?
Brandy: That's a good question, because it's something I need to deal with right away. I think I'm intimidated by authority figures. I see them as being on this pedestal and I'm not their equal at all, and I am not worthy of them. So I think it's insecurity on my part thinking that their time is worth more than to sit down and talk to me, because I don't really have anything to say anyway.

Jennifer: It is important to talk with professors, but I guess I'm not the kind of person who can just drop in on a professor and visit, because I feel that this is a busy person. I can't just stop in if I don't have anything to say, if I don't have a direct question, if I don't have a thesis topic to discuss. I can't just go in and say, "Hi."

Sara: I am very reluctant about going to professors and taking their time. I'm at a point where I've become a professor. I'm going to be teaching Hebrew next year, and I know it's attractive to have a student who does very well and who's very interested. It probably would be a good thing for me to go. I know I could give as much to them as they can give to me. But I still feel like a fourth grader, a very bright fourth grader, but I'm still a fourth grader. I still feel like a little kid, and I'm always afraid that I'm not going to know the right thing to say. Now I'm getting a lot more savvy about that.

Martha: I can remember when I found out my parents were getting divorced, I had a class and it was called Great Books, and we started reading Homer, and we raced through the great books, and I loved that class. There were only six of us in the class and I was always prepared. I had an opinion about everything. And then I couldn't do it anymore. Once that news about that divorce came, I had nothing to say about any of the books. After about two weeks, I went to see the professor to apologize to him because I felt like he had in some way come to depend on me. I walked into his office and said, "I'm really sorry that I haven't been able to participate in class." And he said, "Yeah, I sensed something was going on. Do you want to talk about it?" And I couldn't. The minute he said, "Do you want to talk about it," I thought I would burst into tears. I couldn't believe somebody cared.
Pam: Are you sorry that you didn't talk to him?
Martha: I'm really sorry that I didn't talk to him.
Pam: How come?
Martha: When I look back, so many professors have made themselves available to me, and I couldn't do it. He was really fatherly, really loving, really, really loving.
Pam: Why weren't you able to reach out to them?
Martha: I was so afraid of who I was, of the truth about my family, about how I'd been treated by my father. I felt really unworthy of anybody's time or attention. And I hadn't had a lot of people in my life who could just be really interested in me.

Other women were not afraid of authority but still did not seek out mentors because they had learned to "do it on their own." After all these years, independence had become part of their personal style. Since they did not have guidance in high school, and since they had very little guidance from their parents, they learned to take care of themselves.

Donna: Now that we're talking, I'm realizing how I isolate myself. I know people would have group meetings and make individual appointments with the guidance counselor, but I did it all on my own. I never really relied on anybody else. I never really sought out their advice or anything like that.

Whether or not a student has a mentor is important beyond the need for guidance. For example, being able to attract a mentor is associated with the student's image of competence and can positively affect her self-esteem. In college and graduate school, if a student has attracted the attention of a professor, it is assumed that she is good and has something special to offer. Many students attract mentors because professors like and support their work. In these situations, the student's ideas are validated. Ultimately, women blame themselves for their inability to seek out and attract mentors. They do not experience it as a comment on their independence, they experience it as a rejection of their ideas and their abilities. One of the participants claimed that she knew many women who felt they had something special to offer but whose talents were never recognized. These women probably do have something wonderful to offer, but most people have no way to know that. Since these women are shy about selling themselves, they wait for professors to magically recognize their talents, hoping that somehow a paper, a set of grades, an interesting research idea will draw attention. Sometimes this does happen; most often it does not.

One reason that professors do not always recognize the talents of these students is because when they do seek protégés, they usually look for students who have impressive records. Women like those who were interviewed for this book may not seem impressive when they are evaluated by traditional standards. For example, most of the women in this book did not attend prestigious universities as undergraduates, their standardized test scores were average or slightly above average, and their grades may have suffered slightly in college or in high school because they had to work full-time or because they had family responsibilities. In other words, when professors do seek out students, the women in this book may not stand out as exceptional, though actually they are exceptional.

WHAT MAKES A GOOD MENTOR

Not only is it important to have a mentor, it is important to have a good mentor. Most of my participants wanted three things from their mentors. First, they wanted a mentor who truly cared about them and believed they were smart and special. In other words, they wanted someone who valued what they brought to the plate and was convinced that they did quality work.

Jackie: My advisor was supportive in the sense that she seemed to think without any reservations that I was really good and that I could do really good work, and I always had this feeling when I was in grad school that the emperor had no clothes, and I think it was because I had such a rough time as an undergrad that I really had a lot of doubts about whether or not I was capable of doing graduate education.

They wanted someone who could see beyond traditional evaluation methods to recognize what they had to offer.

Shirley: My mentoring with U.C. Irvine was terrific. I am extremely grateful to my committee chair there. He was wonderful. Let's see—what else has he done? He let me into the program, which was more than anyone else there was willing to do. When I applied, the basis for letting people into the program is that you meet certain minimum requirements, but then someone has to be willing to work with you. So they send your file around and at one point I had all "maybes." But my advisor was willing to take a chance on unconventional students, students who don't necessarily look promising. And some of them turn out well and some don't. I don't know what his criteria is. I'm sure he has some, because I have seen him refuse to work with some students.

Second, the women felt more comfortable with mentors who believed the relationship was reciprocal, not simply a handout. They wanted to be treated like a colleague. The women I interviewed often considered themselves mature beyond their age and did not feel as inexperienced and naive as other students in their programs appeared to them. Some nontraditional students (especially those who are older) are uncomfortable with a student-teacher relationship where the student is presumed to know nothing and the teacher serves as a pitcher of information that can be poured into an empty vessel. This philosophy of teaching was called the banking system of education by Paulo Freire (1970) and the negative effects it has on students was explored in his book *Pedagogy of the Oppressed*. The women in this book did not want to be treated in a way that invalidated their knowledge and their experience. This finding was upheld in another study where it was determined that women want to be recognized for what they already know before admitting what they do not know (Clinchy, et al., 1985).

Pam: So your education was good in graduate school?
Jackie: Yeah, well, first of all, the way they treat graduate students at Berkeley versus undergraduate is like night and day. Undergraduates are shit. The assumption of undergrads is that you're basically a moron until you prove otherwise. The assumption for graduate students is that you're not a moron until you prove otherwise.
Pam: So were you treated like a colleague?
Jackie: Or a junior colleague, but the assumption was that you definitely had potential. It's not like if we turn our backs you're going to start drooling on yourself, which is kind of always the impression I got when I was an undergrad at Berkeley. Particularly in the sciences, because it's such a dick thing. In graduate school, people were very supportive and very kind.

Donna: My assumption is that we're future colleagues and obviously in this school, their assumption is that I'm more powerful than you. I just don't get that, and I didn't get it with Professor X. That's so indecent and, again, I've never got that treatment in my undergraduate program. I never got that at Harvard. And since I've been here, I've been treated so inhumanely.

Finally, and not surprisingly students wanted mentors who were like them. This usually meant for example, that women of color who came from disadvantaged backgrounds wanted mentors who were women of color who came from disadvantaged backgrounds. It is important to recognize the underlying assumption behind this desire, which is that mentors who have backgrounds similar to their students will share similar ideas. The catch here is that this is not always true. Sometimes mentors who have different histories and ethnic identities will share similar ideas and attitudes with students even if they have dissimilar backgrounds. Ultimately, the women I interviewed wanted mentors who understood and appreciated their ideas. They wanted someone who was "like them" in attitude and orientation. Interestingly, a few of the women in this book found the most supportive mentors among older white men who came from privileged backgrounds.

SUMMARY AND DISCUSSION

Protégés and mentors are often attracted to each other because they are similar. Since women from nontraditional backgrounds are in a minority, it is difficult for them to find mentors who are similar in attitude and orientation.

Also, mentors often choose protégés according to traditional criteria, including grades, test scores and past attendance at prestigious institutions. Often, women from disadvantaged backgrounds do not earn the highest grades, they usually do not receive the most notable test scores, and they rarely go to expensive, private, well-known schools as undergraduates. Therefore, these women are often overlooked.

It is important to emphasize that whether or not a protégé has a mentor is important beyond the help and support mentors provide, it is often considered a symbol of the student's competence. Students who can attract "great" mentors are often considered "great" students. This is another way that students from disadvantaged backgrounds are placed in a bad position. Specifically, the cycle of the "old boys' network" is subtly perpetuated. This perpetuation is encouraged not only by mentors who do not recognize talent, but also by protégés who do not know how to sell themselves and connect with a mentor.

7

POSITIVE ASPECTS OF SCHOOLING

In this chapter I talk about what the women liked about their education. In the next chapter, I talk about what they didn't like about their education. If the chapters were reversed, giving the initial impression that the women were angry and didn't really appreciate the assistance they had received, someone would probably get annoyed. Expressing anger in this way is often considered inappropriate and disloyal, even if the criticism is meant to be constructive. In fact, in a conservative climate, some believe that disadvantaged children should be grateful for any help that others are gracious enough to offer. Even from a liberal perspective, those who have worked hard over the last 30 years to make education more accessible would be discouraged to hear only angry criticism, although they would probably understand the reasons for it. The truth is we have come a long way in providing equal opportunity, but there is still a lot to be done. This book stands as a testament to the success of those who have made efforts to provide opportunities for disadvantaged children, but also as a reminder that we have a long way to go before equity of opportunity is a true reality. Those who want to hear how society has helped these women would not be disappointed in their testimonies.

Debbie: It's really weird to have to formulate this stuff as we're sitting. The first thing that I come up with is that it blows my mind what an impact my education has had on my life. My God, I don't know what I would have done without it!

Helen: My education itself has been good. This has really been the key for me. This is the reason that I was attracted to your appeal. I still have that feeling about it, too. I firmly believe in the whole idea of lifelong education, and it's something that always has value one way or another. Some of it's practical and some of it's not so practical, and some of it's just food for thought. It has been a key, and so I think that's the important aspect of it. So UCLA's a good school and I got a lot out of it. The community college that I went to, in its own way, was also a very good school. My high school in its funny kind of way was a good school because I was there. It meant that I had it. It was all part of my development.

In fact, a few women claimed they never had disadvantages; all they had were opportunities.

Janus: I don't think you have barriers. I didn't have barriers; I had opportunity, and I think I had people letting me know that I had opportunity. Therefore I didn't have barriers. I think if I had any barriers, they were barriers after I got in other situations, after I became an adult, and I think that's when I was faced with some barriers that were preventing me from doing certain things.

After reading this chapter and then the next, you will witness the contradictory feelings these women had about their education. It is common for people to criticize an institution while also feeling grateful. My interviews reflected these contradictions. At one time, the women felt grateful as they remembered opportunities. At others times, they were angry as they remembered injustice.

In the previous two chapters, I talked about teachers and mentors. The presence or absence of good teachers and mentors was such an important part of these women's educational experience that I chose to place these topics in chapters by themselves. This chapter (and the next) focus on other aspects of schooling.

THE IMPORTANCE OF EDUCATION

What role did the school play in these women's resiliency? School was often used by the women as an extended or alternative family, a way out of their situations at home and a way to build self-confidence. Education gave them the opportunity to change their lives. When calling to participate in this project, many of the women said the reason they volunteered was that they wanted to tell people how important their education was to them.

When asked why they achieved at their current level, many of the women credited family members; others credited their own perseverance and motivation. Still, when asked what outside force assisted them, many agreed that school was most influential. This is important because education provides one of the few ways for women to be successful and empowered. In the past, women have had fewer opportunities to be as successful as men. They have not had as many opportunities to play professional sports, to take over the family businesses, to become entertainers or to work in high-paying jobs (e.g., unionized factory jobs) that don't require advanced education. Another reason it is important to acknowledge the influence of education is that although other professionals such as doctors and clergy are often credited for having a significant impact on people's lives, educators are not. Teachers are still undervalued. For these women, education significantly impacted their lives.

When schools were successful in accomplishing their goals, it was a source of empowerment for these women. If fact, most of them felt that school became too important because achieving academically became their only source of self-esteem. This caused them to lose sight of the bigger picture. Students chose to engage in activities that would build their self-esteem as opposed to engaging in activities that were "good for them," but perhaps also a little hard on their egos (eg., difficult math classes).

Jackie: The only thing that I felt that I could really do well was school, which meant that as long as I was alive, I wasn't going to give that up because that was the only thing that I was worth a damn at. It wasn't clear to me until I got to college and I wasn't getting A's anymore how much of my worth as a human being was based upon getting an A. That was the only measure of my right to be a human being, the fact that I could continue to get A's. In the face of all kinds of absurdity, I could get A's.

Toni: My identity is tied up in my education. It's really a big deal.
Pam: How is your identity tied up in your education?
Toni: It justifies me, legitimizes me, defines me. What do you do when you have an educational system for a lot of people that is like a train that they jump on that defines them, and the system creates this judgmental system that ranks them and gives them legitimacy?
Pam: So you don't see that as a good thing?
Toni: I really don't. I really don't think it's a good thing. It's too weighted. It's like I'm living for that grade. I'm living for that degree and it closes you off from deeper aspects of yourself.

Many felt that school was the only way out of their situations. When they were young, these women seemed to understand that alternative lifestyles existed elsewhere. Doing well in school empowered these women to believe they could change their lives. It allowed them to be open to other possibilities.

Janet: I don't think that school was necessarily an escape for me, but it was definitely an area where I thought, I've got to succeed at this. I've really got to excel at this because this is my ticket out. I can either be a slut and get married or I can be really smart and work my way out of this. And I decided to take that route.

Helen: I remember one of the things that would kick off a daydream with me was to hear a train whistle in the distance. I would wonder where those people were going. They're going somewhere—they're going off to New York City, and what were they doing there? And I'd think, "Here I am and I'm not going and I really would like to go, and am I ever going to be able to find out what other people do and what the rest of the world is like?" Going to school seemed a way to find out, and to give me a key to the things I wanted to do. So it was definitely important.

Other disadvantaged children that I have been associated with either through my work or through my private life often have an attitude that there is no better life for them. They believe they are trapped in their world and they will never escape. In fact, many do not understand that they function within a certain type of "world." It is as though they believe that everyone experiences the same existence (unless, of course, you are rich; then privilege is magically bestowed upon you). Other realities do not truly exist unless you are one of the lucky (rich) few. The women I interviewed believed that by achieving in school (which was possible), they could change their lives.

School also became an extended family for these women. Teachers played a major role in elementary school. In high school, other students became important. In fact, high school girls will often seek attention from boys as a substitute for the attention they do not receive at home. This can lead to an unhealthy type of emotional dependency that perpetuates the cycle of dysfunction when young girls get pregnant and marry the wrong boys at a young age. The women in this book were able to avoid this type of entanglement with boys. Seeking attention from boys is one way women extend their family into the school culture. At other times, the school replaces the family entirely.

Sara: One day my mother called me up and said, "I'm sorry I was never there for you." And I said, "Well, you weren't there for me, but that's okay because school was there for me." And she was disappointed, and I felt bad about that, but I had transferred all my emotional neediness to school, and it was met, thank god. The teachers loved me, so I got all the rewards that I needed from school. Therefore, it didn't bother me that my family didn't really reward me, because I was getting all that I needed at school.

Ultimately, for the women in this book, education was an important part of their lives. It provided a family, the opportunity to change their future and the means to build confidence.

DISADVANTAGES: NOT ALWAYS BARRIERS

Understanding Individual Barriers

Many of the women faced disadvantages that have been identified in the past as serious barriers for students. For example, some were second-language learners, and few would argue that being unfamiliar with English places children in the United States at a disadvantage. Yet none of the second-language learners in this book emphasized their problems with learning English. Does this mean that language barriers are not important? Probably not. There were reasons why language was not a significant barrier for these women. Maria had grandparents who lived at home and helped her every night with her English. Anne learned English before emigrating to this country. So it is important to recognize that different barriers (even well-recognized ones like needing to learn English) affect people differently depending on personal experience.

This is important because educators should not only address barriers, but understand how these barriers affect individual students. Four of the five women of color in this book claimed they were not seriously affected by race-related issues. The Asian-American woman I interviewed was raised in Hawaii. Janus, a black woman, was raised in Washington, D.C. The degree that women were affected by race depended on where they lived as children, their family's response to race and their own experience with racism.

In many cases, school interventions assist students who need the least amount of help. In response, some minority-group members have fought affirmative action policies because they believe this type of assistance was unnecessary for them and unfair to others (Rodrigues, 1990). They fear that their colleagues will attribute their success to afirmative action policies rather than their own abilities. It has been argued that this creates an atmosphere where minority students must constantly demonstrate competence above and beyond what is expected of others.

Financial barriers caused tremendous problems for some women and did not present a significant barrier for others. Debbie claimed that the plain old financial stuff had been a tremendous obstacle because she'd always had to work while she was in school. It bothered her that she was never able to focus solely on her coursework. She also felt that if she'd had the time to engage in extracurricular activities, she would have gotten to know other people of like minds. In other words, she would have appreciated having time to create an intellectual community around herself.

On the other hand, Michelle claimed that she didn't have any problems with finances in college because she was provided with insurance money from her father, who died when she was in high school. She was able to afford a small, private liberal arts college with the help of her father's endowment.

Addressing Individual Barriers

As the women in this study talked about their experiences, they described situations where schools were successful in addressing individual barriers. First, those who attended smaller colleges received more individual attention.

Pam: How did you like Dartmouth?
Michelle: I loved it. It was great. We had a really small department. There were only 12 professors and about the same number of grad students over all four years. I had a great advisor, he was really good. We had really nice facilities, had a gorgeous office. I had my own office. The campus was beautiful, stereotypically Ivy League with the white steeples, and it was in a small town. Also, I managed to get my Ph.D. in four years. They support you for the full four years.

Those who attended small schools could usually name at least one person who was there for them when they needed help. They felt that the officials cared about them as individuals. This is not meant to suggest that people who teach at small colleges care about their students while those who teach at large universities are incapable of caring. Smaller liberal arts colleges often value teaching and advising at least as much as research. At research universities, a professor's intellectual ability (which is usually demonstrated through publications) is often valued more than his or her ability to be a moral professional who cares about teaching and mentoring students and who works hard to develop positive relationships with colleagues. Just as students will rise to expectations, professors will also rise to expectations. If universities value teaching and mentoring as much as they value research, professors will make the time to develop caring relationships.

Teresa: So what I had at Berkeley was a calm, nurturing, supportive group of people that not only knew who I was as a student, but knew who I was as a person—and cared about that.

Janus: I think the caring part at UVA was probably the one thing that made me go there. I came down to visit and they would just call to make sure everything was okay. They wanted to know what they could offer in the way of support. They considered my daughter and what school she would attend in junior high school, and what high school she would be able to go to. They were always there with me. I mean in everything—it was my advisor.

June: I liked this graduate program because it's very personal. Everybody knows everybody, and I would say that about St. Mary's too. Professors—you get a more personal relationship with them. It's small, so you do social things together, and it's like being in a family for two years. You're with all the same people, all the time. So it's very, very supportive.

The women were also happy in schools where students were encouraged to find and express their personal voices. Writing became an effective way for women to express their voice, but also they expressed voice through art, music and athletics.

The women also provided examples of how schools made them feel welcome as nontraditional students.

Helen: Once we got here and had been living here for a while and realized that California valued higher education enough to actually make it cheap enough for a lot of people to go who wouldn't ordinarily be able to go, and also the community colleges were just being started, which meant that you could go to college while you were working at a full-time job, I decided to go back.

Pam: Can you name one thing that helped you to achieve?
Shirley: One enormous thing that I think is extremely important is the willingness of first-rate universities to accept nontraditional students—I think, particularly for women, coming back at an older age and doing things that you wish you could have done or didn't get a chance to do at the appropriate age. U.C. Irvine was wonderful about that. There

were students there who are older than I am, enough of them that I didn't feel unusual or out of step or anything. And that's not true at other places.

Being dedicated to nontraditional students may seem like an obvious obligation for a school to fulfill, but it is not. People do not all agree that education should provide equal opportunity. For example, Carnoy and Levin (1986) claim that

schools are conservative institutions. In the absence of external pressures for change, they tend to preserve existing social relations. But external pressures for change constantly impinge on schools even in the face of popular tastes. In historical periods when social movements are weak and business ideology is strong, schools tend to strengthen their function of reproducing workers for capitalist workplace relations and the unequal division of labor. When social movements arise to challenge these relations, schools move in the other direction to equalize opportunity and expand human rights. (Carnoy & Levin, 1986, p. 41)

One way for schools to show that they are dedicated to educating diverse students is to provide programs and interventions for nontraditional students. Maria was involved in a program called Inroads, and Janus was involved in a program called Upward Bound. They described these as follows:

Maria: I also got into an organization called Inroads, which is a group here in San Francisco, but it's a national group that works with Latinos, African Americans and Native Americans, and it takes students who are bound to four-year universities that want to work in business or engineering, and if you're accepted you interview with different corporations and you work with the corporation while you're in college during the summer and during your break. And so here I was interacting with business people and I was like 18, and I hadn't even started college yet. They do a lot of training on etiquette, how to do this, how to do that, things that really rounded out what I already had. So that also encouraged me.

Janus: Upward Bound is on the campuses of university settings. You're taught by university professors, and you're given counselors. You stay on campus during the summer and you go Saturdays and some evenings after school. It is a pretty big part of your life during high school, at least I thought it was. I think Howard's program was my greatest influence because that's where I sort of came into my own. I felt like I was pretty independent and powerful in my own right as a 16-17-18-year-old student, because we had rights. We had our own community, and we had our own inauguration and our balls and stuff like that. At that time, I just assumed I was going to college, but I could not go away because I had a baby.

Other participants claimed that involvement in giftedprograms in the early grades helped them to believe they were special from an early age. Most participants believed, however, that the school's commitment to special programs usually did more to illustrate to them that their school was dedicated to educating diverse students then it did to really help them as individuals. This may have been because most programs for nontraditional students are designed to help students who are doing poorly in school or who are ethnic minority students.

Participants also mentioned that they benefited from schools that made an attempt to include curriculum that touched upon their personal experience. This was especially true for the women who had benefited from women's studies and ethnic studies classes.

Joy: When Professor X was an undergraduate student, she found that random samples were random samples of White, Anglo-Saxon, Protestant, 35-year-old heterosexual, middle- to upper-income men—end of story. There were no Blacks, no Jews, no Latinos, no lesbians or gays. There were no women, and this was not the psychology of the people. This was the psychology of white, Anglo-Saxon, Protestant, overweight, 35-year-old white males. And I loved that. I had never known that. That made all the sense in the world to me. That psychology isn't about me. This history class isn't about me. No wonder I thought this was garbage all along. It had nothing to do with me. It wasn't about my dad with his seventh-grade education. It wasn't about my friends with their inner-city Black upbringing. It wasn't about any of us. That's why we thought it was all garbage. And that's how I feel about standardized tests. This isn't about me. I'm not a seventh grader from Cedar Falls, Idaho. I'm not white, middle-class, corn-fed, heartland America. This isn't about me, and there's no way it's about any of my students.

To summarize, the women were satisfied with their schools when they were given the opportunity to have voice, made to feel welcomed in the schools and provided with curriculum that touched on personal experience. Right now words such as "narrative,""dialog" and "voice" are considered popular buzz words in the field of education. The use of these words demonstrate how education has started to aknowledge the importance of open communication embedded in critical reflection. In this book, I attempt to give voice to a certain population of women, and I am not the only social scientist who has talked about giving voice to the voiceless (McElroy-Johnson, 1993). Others have argued that African Americans, Native Americans and Hispanic Americans haven't had a voice in many areas. Also, some people argue that teachers do not have a voice in the transformation of schools and children don't have a voice in their learning process. What does it mean to have voice? People want to feel as though they are understood. Those who feel they are different (usually because they are in a minority) want to feel that other people understand their "different" ideas, concerns, needs and desires. They want people to understand their identification with certain groups while also recognizing that they are individuals who do not want to be stereotyped. They want to feel that their perspectives (or perspectives of people who are "like them") are thoroughly integrated into the culture of the programs they are involved in. For many women, having voice means that they want to be heard. They want to feel their opinions and ideas are respected enough to be taken seriously. They want to have the freedom to write or speak in a manner that represents their true self (not as has been dictated by outdated academic guidelines or other elitist protocols). Some may believe voice is another word for power. Yet I have found that many women don't necessarily want people to change as a result of understanding and acknowledging their perspectives; they just want to know their ideas are being considered seriously. They want to believe that what they have to say is being understood, respected and used in other people's decision-making processes. Ultimately, gaining power might be a result of having voice, but that doesn't seem to be the goal of women who seek to find their voice. The women in the book provide the following examples of situations where they felt their voices were silenced.

Shirley: Once I had a history teacher in high school and some of the things I was saying in her class were very contradictory to her own beliefs. When she found out that I had high scores on the SATs she was upset because then she might have to admit that I might be right, and she didn't like that.

Debbie: I feel like I've really learned to fight to have a voice. Sometimes I think that has been ill received, particularly in graduate school, because I was one of the people who said what was on my mind a lot. I felt like I had to, and I got a great education because of that. But I didn't feel welcomed in that. I assume that's sexism.

Michelle: I speak up less than a lot of people, especially the men. That's sort of my impression—that the men, whether they have something to say or not, will speak up. I won't speak up until I think it's really important and it hasn't been said by someone else and it doesn't look like anybody else is going to say it and I think it's a good point. Otherwise, I'll hold back.

Diane: I should go to him and I should feel comfortable going to him, but I didn't, and that's typical of subordinates in organizations. Many people complain about their jobs but never talk to their supervisors and do something about it. So it's the same type of mentality. For the most part, I don't have a problem voicing my opinion, but—once in awhile, I have felt that it wouldn't have done any good. I felt like it would have done me more harm than good, and after talking with other peers in the program, I decided to just keep my mouth shut and get through it.

SUMMARY AND DISCUSSION

How important was the school in promoting resiliency for these women? School provided a way to build self-confidence, a secure place away from negative home situations, and an extended family. While the women's personalities and intelligence allowed them to take advantage of their opportunities, the school provided the opportunities they needed. In elementary school, early messages that they were smart and special helped them to believe they could change their unhappy situations.

It is not only important to understand the barriers students face, it is also important to understand how each barrier affects individual students. For example, it was found that problems associated with learning English as a second language did not pose a serious barrier for the second-language learners in this project. This does not mean that language barriers are trivial; it means that for the second-language learners who were interviewed, learning a second language was less stressful than other barriers. Knowing how different barriers affect different students is just as important as knowing what barriers exist.

Some of the women believed that going to a small college where people knew them as individuals and cared about them alleviated the effects of their disadvantage. They also suggested that schools should try to understand and value diversity, encourage women to find their own voices and provide opportunities for women to connect their education to their personal experiences.

8

NEGATIVE ASPECTS OF SCHOOLING

While education helped the women I interviewed in many ways, some of their educational experiences made their achievement process more difficult. If we understand how school experiences can be negative even for high achievers, it may be possible to understand why women with backgrounds similar to the women in this book often leave the system. Many of the women I interviewed indicated that although they made it through the process, they could understand why others did not. As I stated earlier, the participants believed that their achievement process was unnecessarily difficult.

Many people believe that college should be a time to have fun; students live off money sent from home, concentrate on their studies and spend most of their free time socializing with friends. This perhaps is the way it should be, but it is not the experience that most nontraditional students have. Once when I told someone that I was a doctoral student, he turned to me and said, "You should try the real world, it's not that bad." I looked at this man with disbelief. He was making the assumption that I had spent 10 years in school leisurely milling around the library contemplating the meaning of life. Actually, by the time I started to get my Ph.D., I already had 10 years of experience as a classroom teacher. Most of my education (including my undergraduate degree) was earned by going to school full-time at night after working a full workday. This was typical of the women I interviewed. Diane was finishing her graduate degree while also working at three "professional" part-time jobs. She told me that she worked from eight in the morning until 10 at night, seven days a week, and I believed her. She was so restless while we talked that I could hardly get her to sit still. At one point, we talked as we walked to the drugstore because she needed to pick up medicine. I could tell that she needed to accomplish two tasks at one time.

Education was not a time of fun and fancy for Diane or for most of the other women interviewed. Many had positive educational experiences, especially in the early grades, but most admitted that some portion of their education or early professional experience was difficult, and at times traumatic. There was at least one woman who was an exception to this rule. Michelle went to a supportive, private liberal arts college as an undergraduate. Then she went to a small, private Ivy League school as a graduate student. After getting her doctoral degree, she received a wonderful postdoctoral fellowship. Michelle would probably claim that she had a positive educational experience throughout most of her schooling. Although she had a traumatic experience as a child with her dad's illness and death, she was able to use his social security money to pay her way to college. This was unusual, however. For most of the women, the educational process was long and arduous.

VALUING DIVERSITY: ACCEPTANCE OF NONTRADITIONAL STUDENTS

One reason the women believed school was difficult was that they very often found that difference was not valued in the academy. The women believed that valuing diversity needed to go beyond minority recruitment and multicultural education. For nontraditional students to feel welcome, programs need to accept and value older students, hire women who are gay, and appreciate the style, attitude, speech patterns and ideas presented by African-American females who are expressively Black. The participants believed that schools do not value diversity when they grudgingly hire or admit women and minorities into a department because affirmative action forces them to do so. In their definition, valuing diversity meant having a real appreciation for what nontraditional students, faculty and women in business can offer to the organization.

Janus: As much as people say that they're hiring minorities–be they women, be they Japanese, be they Black, be they Chinese, or whatever; I don't find that they actually use those individuals for what they have to offer. They only want them as a representative.

For the Caucasian women, valuing diversity meant having others recognize that they were nontraditional students. These women often felt that they were different and yet they were treated as if they were not. They allowed this assumption to continue because their intuition told them that diversity was not valued. However, most agreed that they would rather be respected and valued for who they really are than feel they must act like someone else.

Expensive, private, Ivy League or Ivy League–like schools should be most careful about their reputation. In these schools, students from disadvantaged backgrounds often feel alienated, believing that all the other students come from wealthy and supportive backgrounds. This assumption is most likely untrue. However, it is easy to see how ideas like this can be perpetuated. For example, a large number of the participants had applied to one expensive private school in California and were rejected. This may have been a coincidence. What was interesting, however, was that most of the participants who were turned down believed they were rejected because of their backgrounds. One reason for this was that this particular school asked applicants if their parents (or any other relatives) had attended this university previously. It also asked what their parents did for a living. This led the former applicants to believe that the school was interested only in students whose family members were alumni and could provide money to the school. This could well be a false assumption, but it is important to remember that the people who were questioning this school's integrity were highly educated and successful women. What might others who have less experience think? If schools want a reputation for attracting diverse students, they need to avoid a reputation for bias and project a genuine attitude of openness.

SEXISM

In our society, women still do not earn four-year college degrees, seek majors in science and math and go on to graduate school as often as men (Fisher-McCanne, McCanne & Keating, 1980; Wilson & Boldizar, 1990). In this project, older women mentioned problems associated with sexism more often than younger women. For example, many of the older women described problems they encountered as children with gender expectations that discouraged them from pursuing male-dominated professions.

Debbie: The myth that women don't use their education anyway (they marry educated, rich men instead) was still pervasive when I was young, so there was no preparation for professional achievement.

The younger women (especially those in their early to middle twenties) felt they had experienced less overt sexism.

Problems with sexism were most often brought up by women who were in male-dominated fields, including business, architecture and philosophy. In those fields, women still faced a male-oriented culture that was uncomfortable and restricting.

When women did describe gender issues, they more often described problems related to work rather than those related to school. A few of the participants were surprised at how sexist the work world was after they had been led to believe in school that gender equity was a problem of the past. This was true especially for women who worked in academia, business or in the religious community.

Sara: I sometimes feel that I've crossed the gender line. I've had professors who didn't think highly of female students, for example, really traditional guys who would take me under their wing. I'm a self-identified feminist. I don't have a problem with it. I wanted to be a priest when I was five years old, and I was told that I couldn't because I was a girl, and I said, "What do you mean I can't because I'm a girl?" I think the reason men accept me is because I've had good academic training, that I can think like a man when I want to. I can be a philosopher or I can be a theologian and—
Pam: Talk about Plato or Aristotle.
Sara: Exactly, I can deal with them on their own turf. But that doesn't mean that I have to stop being a woman. It does, however, put them more at ease that I can talk about abstract things like grammar or philosophy. But it's a very strange thing, Professor Y was the same way. He's definitely not a progressive person. He's extremely conservative as far as religion goes. I think his real feeling is that women belong in the kitchen raising babies, and yet he was perfectly willing to work with me as his student.
Pam: There are a few smart women and you were one of them?
Sara: Exactly, I'm one of the acceptable women because I can do the stuff that men can do.

ARROGANCE AND ELITISM

Many of the women mentioned their discomfort with arrogance and elitism in higher education. Society is stratified and so is the school system. A high level of self-esteem, above-average intelligence and a little luck are often mistaken for brilliance and used as an excuse for arrogance and impatience toward those who are not seen as worthy. The people at the top of the educational hierarchy have power, and those on the bottom do not. It is certainly not fair to say that all people in responsible positions in academia are elitist or arrogant. However, the strong hierarchy in academia allows those who are, to demonstrate these behaviors with impunity. Discomfort with arrogance and elitism resulting from a hierarchical structure has been documented in other research studies (Clinchy et al., 1985; Marsick, 1985; Saul, 1992; Terenzini et al., 1993) and definitely revealed itself in my interviews as well.

Joy: One of the things that I really liked about Professor X is that in her first lecture she said that John Johnson (name changed) was an idiot. Anybody who starts a lecture like that is cool by me. She studied under him, and as far as I'm concerned, anybody who would change their name to John, son of John, obviously has a problem to begin with.

Sara: Of all the people in our Department, I picked Professor X as my advisor, and he picked me to be his student, and he's terrible. I mean, he's emeritus now, but he would never have anything to do with the rest of the department. His students never got any money. He never got any grants. He didn't apply for grants. It was like he was above it all. He was a Nobel Prize–winning poet.

Shirley: I was once arguing with this guy who was identifying with Einstein. I realized this afterwards, and I think probably all male physicists identify with Einstein. At one point when we were discussing the "great man" theory versus science as a collective effort theory, I was espousing that in science everyone builds on everyone else. I said that Einstein was in the right place at the right time and that the world was ready for his discovery. And he didn't like that, because he wanted to think of Einstein as this uniquely gifted, special—that his ideas came out of a vacuum. The personal part of it was that if he could think that about Einstein, he was probably at some point cherishing a little view of himself in that way.

Why hasn't hierarchy in higher education been ameliorated? It is possible that this structure works well for people who are raised to admire those who are strong and powerful even if they behave badly? The traditional students are comfortable with a clear chain of command and graciously accept their place as a beginner, realizing that one day they will take their place as a role model. In other words, those in power have gone through the natural progression of first paying their dues and later receiving rewards.

Women who are nontraditional may have more difficulty with this structure. For example, Clinchy and her associates provide a description of a popular development theory in a way that suggests that this style would be undesirable for women. They claim that part of the description of this theory suggests that a

student must stand in judgment and earn the privilege of having (his) ideas respected. Having proved beyond a shadow of a doubt that he has learned to think in complex, contextual ways, the young man is admitted to the fraternity of powerful knowers. Certified as a thinker, he becomes one of Them (now dethroned to lower case "them"). Doubt precedes belief, separation leads to connection. The weak become powerful, the inferiors join their superiors. At traditional hierarchically organized institutions, these places are run by powerful judges charged with forcing the high standards of their disciplines and administering justice through blind evaluation of the student's work without respect to their person. (Clinchy et al., 1985, p. 32)

For nontraditional students and women, it is difficult to look up to those who are part of the dominant class. For example, Fordham and Ogbu (1986) describe the phenomenon they call "acting white." In their theory, Black students may shy away from achievement because they recognize this as a goal of the dominant class. To these students, achieving is a way of assimilating that entails giving up part of themselves. The women in this study may have similar feelings.

In addition, nontraditional students often feel that their hard work and abilities are invalidated. For example, some professionals have argued that accepting students based on affirmative action policies will lower academic standards because underprepared students diminish a teacher's ability to maintain high standards. What has been missing in the affirmative action debate is the acknowledgment that students who face barriers such as discrimination, poverty and stress are probably superior (in many ways) to other students even if standardized test scores don't reveal that fact. It is only logical to expect that students who can overcome barriers and still achieve at levels roughly comparable to their privileged counterparts would indicate ability.

Ogbu (1990) suggests that schools should feel some obligation to adapt their services to different cultures, while the nondominant groups should also make some effort to adapt to the majority culture. He suggests that we should meet halfway and argues that minority students do not have to lose their language or cultural identity to adapt successfully. It is important to recognize, however, that some school cultures are dysfunctional for all students. For example, how many would argue that arrogance is good? The fact that this aspect of school culture is detrimental even to traditional students (though less so than for nontraditional students) suggests that schools should be changed to improve education for everyone.

There are other reasons why the women did not like the hierarchical system now in place. For example, many had learned to question tradition and disagreed with the label of importance that had been bestowed on certain people. They wanted to judge for themselves whether or not an individual deserved respect.

Shirley: If I have respect for someone, it is because they are competent and conscientious and have good values. You know they are meeting standards that I've set for what respect is, and it is not on a basis of age or this guy's got tenure and this guy's the department chair—etcetera.

Jennifer: There are definitely professors that I respect. I respect their intelligence, I respect their insight. But then there are also the blusterers who are just trying to impress whomever with what they say and how much they know. So I guess it takes me some time to decide—is this person worthy of respect or not, and then if they're not, I don't have to worry.

In addition, because people in power do not always value diversity, nontraditional students do not always move through the process from empty vessel to grand leader in a progressive, nonconflictual way. They usually have to struggle and often are denied the opportunity to reach the top positions. Even if they are not denied top positions because of discrimination, many give up before reaching the top because they are so exhausted from the extra work they must accomplish to compete with those from privileged backgrounds. For example, a person from a privileged background may finish graduate school (without ever working outside of school to support herself) at the age of 25; by 30 years old she may be reaping the rewards of money and prestige bestowed upon people who (somehow) have managed to attain their graduate degrees and five years of work experience at such an impressively young age. By contrast, it is not uncommon for nontraditional students to work at low-paying, part-time jobs for 10 to 15 years while struggling to finish school by the time they are 35 years old. At that time, most women are in the midst of raising a family. To be successful, these women must move from working 80 hours a week at a low-paying, difficult job while finishing school to working 80 hours per week in order to get ahead in a new career while also throwing up from pregnancy and changing diapers. Is it any wonder many women give up their dreams to move into top-level positions? Even at this stage, privilege can help women in these situations, as those who can afford housekeepers, gardeners, decent child care and newer cars are much more likely to get ahead in their careers while struggling with balance between hone and career. Some like to point out that women can choose whether or not to become mothers. In response to these pronouncements, it is nice that in today's world, men are well aware of and frustrated with their wives' struggles. Many men no longer want women to choose between career and family. Most need and want their partners to work and they also want children, so, today men are starting to advocate a more equitable balance between family and career. Also, since working women are asking their husbands to accept 50 percent of the child-care workload, more and more men are also starting to experience the difficulties of balancing family with career.

There are other reasons why nontraditional students do not recognize or accept a clear chain of command. Many of the women in this book did not experience a normal and positive chain of command in their families. Even as children, they were often more capable and responsible than their parents. Some believed that in their families, they were the parents and their parents were the children. For these women, the chain of command associated with family roles was experienced as abusive. As adults they felt vulnerable in situations where they were forced to trust people in power. They felt that if people in powerful positions were abusive, those on the bottom would have no recourse. For example, if a graduate student could not get along with her advisor (regardless of whether the advisor was a raving lunatic), this could seriously have affected her ability to get a job. This also happens in dysfunctional families. Children often feel they have no recourse. The only way to survive is to avoid or endure the abuse. Many of the women in this book believed the school system is structured in the same way.

Jackie: What kind of recourse do you have if a professor is unfair? You don't have any recourse. You don't have any recourse as a student. I really feel that people go through enormously painful processes to get their theses done because they're an intimate reflection of yourself. And it's hard to deal with criticism of yourself on that intimate level. And even if it's well intended, and oftentimes, given the egos involved in academia, it's not well intended. Professors are not necessarily the best people in the world. In fact, some have the worst social skills and no sensitivity. Being sensitive and having good social skills is not what gets you tenure. And these people are often easily threatened, and I wouldn't necessarily choose these people as my friends. So, no, I don't think there is recourse. I think in my situation—this professor had suffered abusive situations and often when people experience abuse and don't process it, they end up being somewhat abusive to other people. I think if a professor screws you over, unless you have a really good case and you have a lot of backup, you're tilting at windmills. In fact, you're not only tilting at windmills, you're going to be ruined. You're not going to get a job. I know several people who cannot get jobs for that reason.

Donna: I had a real problem with one of the professors here that was openly discriminating against me because I had a disability. In fact, after I went through this incredibly horrible emotional nightmare with him, I found out that he had done it to several other students and everybody felt powerless.

Martha: There were some professors that I felt really silenced by, the ones that reinforced the message that I wasn't worthy.
Pam: Did you feel that happened a lot?
Martha: I feel like that happened a lot.
Pam: Did you experience this as being abusive?
Martha: When the TA said to me, "What are you, stupid?" I thought that was really abusive. But being yelled at wasn't, I was used to that from my father.

Those who grow up in supportive families (where the chain of command was not abused) are more comfortable with a hierarchical structure in the schools. Even if they have experienced some abuse from educators, this is considered unusual and their attitude toward school can remain positive. Women from stressed families might experience emotional abuse in school as a common occurrence that affects them deeply, reminding them of their lack of control in other situations. They may respond to apparently minor injustices in ways that seem too strong. For example, they may react strongly to a simple and common occurrence such as unconstructive criticism. This reaction may be interpreted by traditional students as extreme. It is important to point out, however, that this response may not be out of proportion in relation to the nontraditional student's own culture of expression. When others indicate that these responses are "too strong," they are judging such a student according to white, middle-class standards. As we judge students according to traditional standards, we send messages that nontraditional students do not belong, or that they must adapt to be accepted.

So far I have talked about why nontraditional students may feel uncomfortable with arrogance and hierarchy, but I haven't talked about the structures in educational institutions that reinforce hierarchy. For example, hierarchy is encouraged through the competitive nature of schooling. In a review article on women in adult education, the authors conclude that women are often characterized in the literature as more able to learn from one another or in a collaborative mode than alone or in a competitive mode (Hayes & Smith, 1994). Others suggest that the competitive nature of math and science fields could turn girls and women away from those fields (American Association of University Women Educational Foundation, 1992). In the current project, a majority of the women claimed they did not like competition, however, a large minority liked competition. What is interesting is that many of those who claimed they liked competition defined competition differently than is usually expected. These women liked competing against themselves, not others. In fact, most did not want other people to do badly, or did not care at all whether others did badly.

Pam: Did you like academic competition?
Anne: Yes.
Pam: Did it motivate you, or—
Anne: Yes. Yes, it did. I didn't want other people to do badly. I just wanted to do very well. I don't care if the whole class has an A. I wanted to have an A, too, or at least do well.

Those who didn't care, only cared about doing well themselves. It is important to understand that for people to compete against others, they must first look beyond themselves. These women had so much happening in their lives, they did not care what others were doing; they focused on surviving and achieving, themselves.

Sara: It was probably only at the end of high school that I realized that people thought I was really competitive because I was really focused on getting A's, and, in fact, it was my best friend who told me that—"You know," she said, "well, you're really competitive." And I said, "No, I'm not. I'm not competing with anybody." And she said, "What, everybody in the class is trying to do better than you," and it was like really? I mean, it didn't occur to me that this might be one of the things that people would do.

For those who did not want others to do badly, ultimately they did not enjoy their success because it came at the expense of other people's feelings. It should also be mentioned that many were not competitive with others, especially in elementary school, because they never felt they had any real competition. (This is an example of how these women believed they were extremely smart almost to the point of arrogance while at other times they exhibited low self-esteem.) In elementary school, the women believed that they were always the best; competing against themselves was ultimately the greatest challenge they faced.

As I mentioned before, the women in this project did not always like traditional methods of evaluation, especially standardized tests. In some cases, standardized tests were helpful, allowing students to recognize their talents when they had previously been ignored. But most of the time, they were detrimental. While women were trying to convince themselves they were special, standardized tests were telling them they were not. This group of resilient women found ways to dismiss these and other negative messages. For example, many were well aware of-and emphasized—the philosophy that standardized tests do not measure abilities accurately. Most felt that what they had to offer was not measured on standardized tests. They believed these evaluation tools measured abilities that are traditionally valued in our society, and that they grew out of an oppressive culture. In related studies, researchers have questioned our ability to recognize gifted disadvantaged children using traditional methods of evaluation and believe educators should find alternate ways of measuring children's potential (Baldwin, 1985; Deschamp & Robson, 1984). For example, Baldwin (1985) suggests that we evaluate giftedness as follows: (1) use of colorful, persuasive language with peer group, (2) ability to use commonplace items for purposes other than those intended, (3) ability to remember and report detailed information concerning events that occurred in the community outside of the school and (4) ability to judge environmental situations by cues that are not usually taught in school.

In some cases the women were motivated by standardized tests because they wanted to prove the tests were inaccurate. In other words, whenever a test suggested that they might not be exceptional, rather than believing the result and allowing it to affect their self-esteem, they set out to prove the test was wrong.

Pam: How do you feel about standardized tests?
June: I hate standardized tests. Those were hard for me. I didn't do horribly, but I didn't do very well on them either. I feel like they're not a good depiction of your abilities. I proved how wrong those things are because they would have pegged me as an average student. I showed them!

Joy: I think that standardized tests measure you according to somebody else's continuum, and I don't think there is a norm anymore. I don't think anybody's normal. I'm not sure where they're finding these Nebraskan classrooms, and how they missed out that everybody else has gone to Mars, but they did. I think that everybody really wishes there was a standard and that this was 1950 and cars had fins and we could all pull up to drive-through burger places and the good old days were still here. But I believe that the good old days never existed, and I believe that those corn-fed, heartland, seventh graders who invented the SAT are holding people up to a standard that never really existed and has nothing to do with the gross majority of people's lives.

SUMMARY AND DISCUSSION

The participants provided examples of norms and structures within the school system that discouraged their progress. Many of the problems stemmed from a hierarchical system that encouraged certain behaviors and attitudes. For example, people on the bottom of a hierarchy are often expected to be compliant and to show deference to those in positions above them. People on the top are occasionally (not always) egotistical and arrogant. This structure is offensive to women because they want to be appreciated for what they have to offer. Women in this book believed they had more life experiences than their privileged counterparts and therefore had difficulty accepting the traditional role of a student, a new employee or a low-level professor, who is considered inexperienced and less knowledgeable. Another reason that the women had difficulty accepting a hierarchical structure is that they had often been at the bottom of an abusive hierarchy associated with their families. In these situations, they had no control or recourse for unfair treatment. For this reason, they were uncomfortable when they found this structure replicated in the school system.

Some of the structures that are in place to support the hierarchical system are the elitist way colleges are stratified, traditional testing methods that misevaluate nontraditional students, and competitive rather than cooperative methods of teaching and learning.

9

ACHIEVEMENT AND DEVELOPMENT PATTERNS

I have always been fascinated by the way women are drawn to certain careers. Many more women than men are elementary schoolteachers, social workers, librarians and nurses. In the past, I have accepted the common explanation that women are drawn to "soft" careers because they are socialized to be caring nurturers. I also believe that women have been locked out, either physically or emotionally from other careers that have traditionally been dominated by men. Still, even in the eighties when yuppie parents were trying to fascinate their girls with the laws of physics and periodic tables (the keys to success in the "good" fields), many women continued to be more interested in caring for people. After hearing the women's stories, I came to the conclusion that there may be another reason why girls (at least those from disadvantaged backgrounds) often choose careers that have stereotypically been labeled "feminine."

I believe that resilient girls from disadvantaged backgrounds may develop differently from nonresilient girls or those children who do not face poverty and stress. It is possible they may develop a type of emotional intelligence as an adaptation to stress. Competence in certain areas as the result of an advanced level of emotional intelligence carries them through school and helps them to appear smart and special. This type of intelligence also draws them to subjects where they have intellectual superiority. They are interested in these fields because they have an aptitude for them.

The idea that some children may adapt to disadvantage in a way that could positively affect ability is not new. Carroll (1940) suggested that low socioeconomic status helped to develop ability. He claimed that many children born in a low socioeconomic level owe their later eminence to that fact. Frierson (1965) believed that Carroll 's point of view was anecdotally supported, but suggested that the more widely accepted thesis, based upon research evidence, was that low status obscures ability and prevents the full development of human potential.

It seems obvious 30 years later that both are true. For a few resilient children, barriers can provide motivation. For nonresilient children, barriers discourage achievement. The women in this book believed that a stressful childhood made the achievement process long and arduous, but it also made them stronger people, helped them to better understand others, gave them insights about class and ethnicity, and motivated them to achieve.

The articles written many years ago heralding the abilities of disadvantaged children were often patronizing, suggesting that disadvantaged children (which at the time referred almost exclusively to Black children) were really not as "dumb" as prejudicial stereotypes would suggest. The current project was based on very different assumptions. These women were quite successful.

GENDER DIFFERENCES IN DEVELOPMENT

Although this book does not focus on the developmental differences between boys and girl, it is based on the assumption that differences do exist. Gilligan (1982) claimed that in the past, developmental theory accounted for male, but not necessarily human, development. She believed developmental theory identified the stages of growth toward autonomy but ignored the evolution of the ability to care, share and create community. Gilligan believed that in the past, the problem with the picture of adult development was that critical voices were missing in the traditional theory base, including those of women, people with varying ethnic backgrounds, and persons belonging to different socioeconomic classes (Gilligan, 1982).

Chodorow (1974), a leading scholar on women's development, observes that during early socialization "feminine personality comes to define itself in relation and connection to other people more than masculine personality does," (p. 44). She suggested that the concept of "being" is central to women because they are the primary socializers and nurturers of children; in comparison, "doing" is primary within men's lives because of the centrality of their work roles.

According to Caffarella and Olson (1993), women's development is characterized by multiple patterns, role discontinuities, and a need to maintain a "fluid" sense of self. The importance of relationships and a sense of connectedness to others was seen as central to the overall developmental process throughout a women's life span. Yet there also appears to be a need for women to capture their own spirit of self, to be given recognition not just for being nice, but for abilities and competencies.

Past literature tends to support the theory that women might develop differently than men. Also, the literature suggests that differences between men and women are often associated with the idea that women's development is grounded in attachment and affiliation rather than separateness and autonomy. Boys and girls who come from disadvantaged backgrounds may develop different strengths as a result of adaptation to their environment. I suggest that resilient girls develop what has been described as "emotional intelligence, or inter- and intrapersonal intelligence," which is grounded in attachment and affiliation. Boys might develop what some call "street smarts," which is grounded in separateness and autonomy. Either way, some would argue that in school, teachers often focus on boys' strengths (Sadker & Sadker, 1994).

DEFINING INTERPERSONAL AND INTRAPERSONAL INTELLIGENCE

So far I have suggested that resilient women might succeed because at an early age they develop a highly advanced level of interpersonal and intrapersonal intelligence. The concept of interpersonal and intrapersonal intelligence was developed by Howard Gardner as part of his Theory of Multiple Intelligences (Gardner, 1983). According to Gardner:

In its most primitive form, the intrapersonal intelligence amounts to little more than the capacity to distinguish a feeling of pleasure from one of pain and, on the basis of such discrimination, to become more involved in or to withdraw from a situation. At its most advanced level, intrapersonal knowledge allows one to detect and to symbolize complex and highly differentiated sets of feelings. The other personal intelligence turns outward, to other individuals. The core capacity here is the ability to notice and make distinctions among other individuals and, in particular, among their moods, temperaments, motivations, and intentions. Examined in its most elementary form, the interpersonal intelligence entails the capacity of the young child to discriminate among the individuals around him and to detect their various moods. In an advanced form, interpersonal knowledge permits a skilled adult to read the intentions and desires—even when these have been hidden—of many other individuals and, potentially, to act upon this knowledge." (p. 239)

This set of abilities has also been described in other ways, with slightly different criteria. For example, Goleman (1995) describes a similar concept he calls "emotional intelligence." According to Goleman, emotional intelligence includes self-awareness and impulse control, persistence, zeal and self-motivation, empathy and social deftness. Daniel Goleman and Howard Gardner both argue that the traditional view of intelligence has been too narrow, ignoring a crucial range of abilities that matter immensely in terms of how effectively we function.

PATTERNS OF INTELLECTUAL DEVELOPMENT

The women in this book developed important skills, expertise and interests in certain areas and often lacked basic knowledge in other more traditional areas. Their differences caused them to be evaluated inaccurately because teachers generally expect students to develop in a similar way, especially if they hide their backgrounds and appear to have similar histories.

By the time these women were in graduate school, they wanted to be free to follow their intellectual curiosity and make decisions about what they needed to know. They not only wanted some academic freedom (like most graduate students), they usually considered academic requirements useless and frustrating. I suggest that rejecting requirements might not represent a lower level of development; instead, it could represent a type of rebellion. The women in this study were able to produce according to traditional standards, but in many cases they were unwilling.

The analysis of these women's educational progress suggests that their teachers attempted first to teach them basic skills, such as how to express themselves, how to calculate mathematical equations and how to use proper grammar. Later, they were expected to develop problem-solving skills. At that time they were expected to reflect and connect their knowledge to specific situations. Many of the women in this book showed signs that they had highly advanced levels of thinking at a very young age and were bored with the basic skills curriculum.

As was mentioned before some women claimed they felt they had something to offer, but no one recognized their talents. When asked what it was they had to offer, however, many were unsure. Some claimed to be good writers, others said they were empathic and still others claimed they could relate concepts to specific situations. These descriptions are partial, not fully developed. In the example below, Shirley talks about her ability to use her "talent" to compensate for her lack of skills. Shirley is a highly articulate Ph.D. who is now conducting research at an Ivy League university, but still her description is vague as she compares "talent" and "skills."

Shirley: I know the respects in which I'm exceptional, but the things that I've been able to do, I don't think most people could do, because I've substituted talent for lack of skills that I should have had. And not everybody's going to be able to do that. So they've got to get the skills.

I suggest that the women in this study have developed a higher level of emotional intelligence or inter- and intrapersonal intelligence. However, there are other ways to describe this set of abilities. For example, perhaps these women had a higher level of critical thinking as described by Taylor. In Taylor's (1990) description of the connection between critical thinking and creative thinking, she claims that of utmost importance to critical thinking is organization. Organization helps the learner gather a full and comprehensive picture of the problem—bits and pieces are pulled together. The learner is able to go beyond the given and develop new insights about the problem. Thinking is stimulated and many alternative responses are offered for solutions to issues and events. Critical thinking encourages the learner to seek the missing link in information. While the learner uses critical thinking to explore ideas and concepts, creative thinking is used to produce ideas and concepts. Ultimately, a person becomes aware of a problem, the difficulty or gaps in information for which there is no learned response; formulates, hypothesizes and searches for possible solutions from ones' own past experience; evaluates, modifies, tests and retests these possible solutions and communicates the results to others. (Taylor, 1990, p. 2)

Taylor also claimed that critical thinking requires that the individuals become willing to examine information from a reflective and introspective stance.

I believe the women's ability to think critically resulted from the need to adapt to difficult environments. The reasons their abilities have gone unnoticed are that because they don't always communicate their ideas well and because their teachers often focused on basic skills and content knowledge rather than higher-level thinking. This interpretation is supported by the fact that these women felt much more comfortable in Ivy League or other prestigious universities than they did at less prestigious schools. Not only did those who attended Ivy League schools believe they were treated with more respect, they also connected intellectually with the academic expectations of the school. The women who attended these schools claimed that they did not focus on basic skills, but instead on their ideas and potential. If they were lacking skills in a certain area, the school simply provided extra help in this one area without making them feel inadequate in all areas. The women in this study felt that officials in Ivy League schools looked beyond traditional evaluation methods. As I found in their transcripts, the women in this book usually earned better grades in prestigious schools that have a reputation for being more rigorous, and they earned lower grades in less prestigious schools that have a reputation of being less rigorous.

Joy: I've got two things to say. Harvard was the best thing that ever happened to me. And Harvard's program is not rigorous. Harvard's program is not difficult. You don't have to do anything once you get in, because getting in is really hard. And if you don't do anything, the only person you're cheating is yourself. I've never felt that way about education before. It was always just a roller coaster ride that you get through and then life starts after. I thought Harvard was cool because it was grad school. I thought that grad school was about learning for the sake of learning and what I found out is that Harvard was cool because it was Harvard. Recently, somebody asked me if Harvard was very rigorous, and I said, "No." And he kind of giggled and said, "I knew Harvard wasn't rigorous." And I don't know how to articulate it, but that's not the point. Harvard isn't rigorous. That's not the point.

The women in this book expressed anger at poor evaluation methods and rebelled when educators focused on what could be described as "basic skills." To many of the women, basic skills were considered trivial details that had held them back in the past. They experienced standardized tests and other forms of traditional evaluation methods as a way for "the other" to force them to develop and adapt according to traditional expectations and beliefs. These women experienced basic skills training as the need to jump through hoops. Since they felt that they had already jumped through many more hoops than are expected of others, they had less patience for what they experienced as arbitrary barriers. These women became resentful that educators could not see beyond superficial evaluation methods that classified them on the basis of trivial details rather than on the depth of their ideas. At times, they perceived the professors around them as lacking intelligence. This is especially true when professors provided feedback that was considered trivial (e.g., "this paper is not in APA format"). This has been documented before in other similar studies on women. For example, Clinchy, Belenky, Goldberger and Tarule (1985) gave an example of a nontraditional student whose standards conflicted with her teacher's in a similar way:

when the student wrote out of her own experience, she felt she knew what she was talking about, but the teacher felt the paper wasn't about anything. When she pasted together a mess of undigested secondhand information, he was satisfied. (Clinchy et al., 1985, p. 34)

It is not my intent to suggest that basic skills are trivial. Most believe they are not. Taylor (1990) points out that for creative thinking, basic skills are important. She believes that the learner's ability to become aware of the problems and gaps in information is critical, but in her opinion, the ability to produce alternative solutions and evaluate those solutions, is based on knowing basic concepts.

What educators need to understand is that women like those in this book might rebel against concerted efforts to improve their basic skills because they believe that what they have to offer is being ignored, invalidated or trivialized. They rebel against being judged according to what others value or consider important rather than what they think is important. Once again, they are being held to the standards of the traditional majority and their talents are being ignored.

Another question to consider is whether or not the women were truly deficient in basic skills. Because these women had exceedingly high standards for themselves and because they believed they were deficient in certain areas, such as in their ability to speak out, to attract mentors, to express themselves, to calculate equations, or to use proper grammar, they often presented themselves as deficient. When they compared themselves, usually they were comparing themselves to other highly successful students in prestigious universities. Their perceptions seemed skewed. For example, Shirley was convinced when she entered graduate school, she was underprepared in math for her courses in statistics. And there is no doubt that she struggled with statistics, had to get extra tutoring, and ultimately earned lower grades in her statistics classes. By the time she was finished struggling with this subject, however, she felt confident in her abilities. It would be interesting to explore whether other students in her program really were much more advanced in their statistics knowledge. It is certainly possible, but what I found interesting was that although Shirley emphasized this particular weakness of hers, she never mentioned the possibility that she might be ahead of her fellow students in other areas. The fact that Shirley won a prestigious four-year postdoctoral fellowship at two major universities after her doctoral program (one in the San Francisco Bay area and one in Boston) would suggest that although she didn't earn A's in statistics, someone recognized her other talents.

I believe the women thought they were deficient because they had a sense that they could have known so much more if they had grown up in privileged circumstances. They believed that privileged children had the opportunity to learn all that they themselves knew, plus all that they missed. This may not be true. Children who grow up in privileged circumstances may use their extra time and energy to have fun while they grow up. They may also use some time to explore other interests (like playing the piano), which could benefit them psychologically and come in handy during the holiday season, but ultimately doesn't help them with their career in medicine or art history.

Still, it is true that because of psychological barriers, lack of guidance, continual moving, or lack of educational resources at certain schools, these women may have been exposed to education that was not as effective as that received by more privileged students. Hirsch (1996) would argue that most children (especially disadvantaged children) have not been taught important content knowledge. Research has shown that there have been striking disparities between sociocultural and economic groups on all standardized tests (Bock & Moore, 1986). These disparities exist even when persons of the same educational level are compared.

Many of the women in this book would claim they were not taught enough content in school, however, many would also claim that they were not taught enough critical thinking. From the women's testimony, I believe that in the lower grades, the schools often focused on basic skills and content knowledge, expecting the children to memorize the names of the planets, the parts of a flower, the parts of the human body and their multiplication tables. Memorizing facts was both easy and boring for these women. In a few rare cases, the women were exposed to better instruction in the lower grades. For example, Joy attended a school that she called "the ashram" which she described as excellent both for teaching content and developing critical thinking. Teresa attended schools over seas where she claimed she was taught to be a scholar. Usually, however, the women's critical thinking skills developed as a result of reflecting on their situations and surviving, even thriving, in difficult situations at home. So, for most of the time, the women believed they did not receive enough instruction in content or critical thinking. What they did get from school was a safe place to interact with caring adults who reinforced the idea that they were smart and special .

Hirsch (1996) argues today that we need a standardized curriculum focusing on specific content knowledge. He believes this knowledge will give disadvantaged children self-esteem and teach them what they need to know to thrive in our society. It seems obvious to me that children need to be taught both specific content knowledge and critical thinking skills. And, I'm sure liberals and conservatives would agree on that point. I think, however, we need to be realistic. It is going to be difficult for schools to teach disadvantaged children all the content knowledge that privileged children receive from their schools and from other aspects of their environment. Teenagers from disadvantaged backgrounds often hold jobs outside of school to earn extra money. At times they have to expend enormous amounts of energy to baby sit, avoid abuse or keep their homes clean. It is common for them to crave emotional support that they satisfy by spending time with friends and lovers. Even if every school in the country was exactly the same, it is a fantasy to believe that schools can equalize the amount and type of content knowledge children are exposed to throughout their childhoods.

What is not a fantasy however, is that children from disadvantaged backgrounds are exposed to important information from their environments that middle- and upper-class children may never experience. If people want to equalize opportunity, they need to capitalize on what poor children bring to their learning process. When school officials accept that children from disadvantaged backgrounds acquire knowledge from their experiences that can be useful in our society, the schools send a message to these children that they are not deficient, just different. Ultimately, when educators rely on standardized tests that measure specific types of content knowledge, they reinforce the idea over and over again that certain children never learn what is important for them to know in our society (and probably never will). In this case, the children's confidence falters and they give up. Shirley said, "I've substituted talent for lack of skills that I should have had. And not everybody's going to be able to do that. So they've got to get the skills." I believe there are many more children from disadvantaged backgrounds who could also use "talent" instead of "skills," but it takes a very sharp educator to recognize a student's talent. Opponents of standardized tests have argued that these tests do not necessarily provide an accurate measure of all the abilities necessary to succeed in our society. I think it is important for people to consider that argument before spending huge amounts of money to force instructors to teach children how to do well on standardized tests.

What ultimately happened with the women in this study is that an advanced level of emotional intelligence allowed the women to do better in social science and humanities because many important theories in these areas are based on information that could be observed directly in their lives, while information about science and math must usually be studied in carefully constructed environments. As a result of adapting to stressful environments, these women had become experts at observing human behavior. Once again, in social sciences these women could rely on their advanced level of inter- and intrapersonal intelligence to help them achieve intellectual superiority in these fields. In a sense they had a "head start" in these fields from their personal experience, whereas in science and math, they start out behind.

Occasionally, as fledgling academics or as students, these women had the experience of developing theories about human behavior based largely on their own personal observations and reflection. In these situations, other professionals often assumed that the women's ideas were based on theories that had been presented elsewhere by experts, when actually these students had independently developed the theories on their own with little or no knowledge of related research. Of course, these women never told anyone who could encourage their potential because they were too modest to tell people the truth about their original ideas. Below, Shirley provides an example of this phenomenon. Notice that at the end of the statement, it is clear that she wanted education professionals to recognize her talents without needing to advocate for herself.

Shirley: I think I can see overall patterns and make comparisons between things that are not obvious to other people. In my very first history class, I took Western Civilization, we had to write a paper, and I wrote a paper and a got a B+ and was astonished because I thought it was an A paper. I'd put a lot of thought into it. And later I found out that the TA said I hadn't taken the ideas far enough, which was a little strange. It struck me as a little strange because I knew that what I'd done was above and beyond the call of duty in terms of the ideas that were in there. Later, what I found out was that the TA was assuming that I had read a book by Robert Graves and that my paper was based on the things that he said in that book. I'd never seen that book, and essentially what I'd done was, I had independently come up with the same idea for how the changes in the city-state in Greece had affected the growth of the arts. The TA had quite rightly said that if I'd read that I should have applied it, so it was a misunderstanding. What I think should have happened was that at some point one of the professors should have noticed that I was doing something different than what most history students do and said something to me. They should have at least asked.

Shirley's quote also illustrates how her thinking was advanced while her basic skills and knowledge may have been lagging. This quote states that the teacher's assistant (TA) thought that Shirley had based her ideas on a history text. Although Shirley had started to develop an insightful theory in her essay, she had never read this particular author which suggests that she did not have a thorough understanding of related literature in the field.

Since it was important for these women to please the teacher, they tended to stick to subjects where they had control over their achievement. They wanted to know that they could accomplish their goals with hard work or talent. In science and math, students must often experiment, deal with confusion and at times handle failure. In these areas, students learn as much from their failures as their triumphs. The women in this book always wanted to know the answer because this is what they were reinforced for in elementary school and because it helped them to compensate for the low self-esteem associated with their nontraditional backgrounds. When they could not be perfect, they shied away from the topic. This reinforced their lack of skill acquisition in certain areas, and it discouraged them from seeking careers in science and math.

These women's strengths and weakness are illustrated well by the following example. If any of the women in this book (since none were engineers) were placed in an engineering seminar and expected to design a human service robot, people might be shocked to discover how well these nonengineers could use and manipulate their limited knowledge. They might be surprised at the women's keen observations of the world, their ability to quickly ask pertinent questions, and their understanding of the potential users of the service robot. However, these women would ultimately not have the tools from math, physics and ctronics to follow through on their ideas and build a robot. It is also possible that their ideas, although outstanding for their level of knowledge, might seem immature because in engineering and in other similar fields, ideas are constrained by knowledge of what is practical or possible given the tools that are available. These women would not know what tools were available. They would lack basic skills.

What ultimately happened with these women is that despite their potential and their hard work, they ultimately achieved at an average (or slightly above-average) level. For this reason they were encouraged occasionally but were rarely given the support that many other high achievers are provided. This was not always due to an actual lack of skills, however, but rather to a perceived lack of skills. Since most of them believed they were deficient, they often presented the image that they were deficient and people judged them according to their level of self-confidence.

Joy: I think when you go to College, you automatically rate yourself on a continuum of the stories that you're hearing. And although I had more radical experiences, they had more of the valued stuff like economics and statistics and things that I can't do. And they had confidence. They believed that they could get that job at USAID because they could do a regression theory. I don't believe I can get that job because I can't do that stuff, and I know I can't do that stuff. I have this self-doubt that a lot of them didn't seem to have. Now, they may all internally have the same self-doubts. They may be thinking look at her, she's a founding mother of special education in Tunisia and I'll never get to do that. And if that's true, I wish they would verbalize that, because it would make me feel better.

As was mentioned before, these women were extremely hesitant to assertively explain to educators their belief that they had something to offer. Often they waited, hoping and praying that someone would recognize their talents. They were unsure of their talent and needed someone else to reassure them before boldly pronouncing their place in the professional world. This stems from modesty and a lack of confidence.

Unfortunately, most teachers did not recognize these women's special talents. Since they did fairly well in academics, teachers were confused. On one hand, the women seem independent and capable; on another hand, they lacked confidence. They earned good grades, yet they produced average test scores. What ultimately happened is that these women were ignored. They were seen as slightly above average and were halfheartedly encouraged to continue, but because people did not recognize or understand their abilities, their exceptional talents went unnoticed or undervalued. Ultimately, their fears were supported and their talent was unrecognized. It seems what these women needed most from their schools was not to be taught to have specific facts on the tip of their tongues, but for the schools to trust that what they had to offer was important and useful.

PATTERNS OF ACHIEVEMENT

Patterns of Achievement in Elementary School Through College

This project provided a unique opportunity to explore the women's achievement patterns between elementary and graduate school. Their achievement patterns were closely associated with their development patterns. Most claimed they enjoyed and excelled in elementary school. Unfortunately, in high school and in college, their feelings were not as positive. To be precise, however, "not doing well" for this population could mean the difference between earning an A average and a B average. For the women in this book, this was the difference between doing poorly and doing well. In graduate school, once again the women did very well academically.

Many of the women claimed that they turned away from academics in high school and then later in graduate school, they became interested in learning once again. This pattern has been described in other projects (American Association of University Women Educational Foundation, 1992; French & Murphy, 1983; Orenstein, 1994).

While the participants were recognized for their accomplishments in elementary school, they became anonymous in high school and college. Many of the women claimed they were recognized in elementary school for two reasons: for being nice, obedient girls and for easily completing academic requirements.

Jennifer: In elementary school, I got good grades. I just did the work and I got good grades. It wasn't so much an effort.

Pam: You got straight A's in school even though you tried to commit suicide, et cetera?
Jackie: School wasn't that hard back then. It really wasn't. It just wasn't. Plus the only thing that I felt that I could really do well was school, which meant that as long as I'm alive I wasn't going to give that up because that was the only thing that I was worth a damn at. But also, it just wasn't difficult back then.

As was mentioned earlier, one of the reasons that elementary school was easy for these women was because they had already developed a high level of critical thinking (emotional intelligence) when they entered school. These higher level skills propelled them easily through the early grades. In the American Association of University Women report (1992), investigators suggest that since girls are ahead of boys in some areas in elementary school, teachers often turn their attention to boys, who need extra help. In these cases, girls are left to move through the required curriculum independently. They do this easily, but they are not challenged to learn beyond what's expected. Later, in high school, when social issues become extremely important to them, they suffer from missing the opportunity to excel in elementary school.

Since these girls thrived on recognition (which was lacking at home), they found other ways to get attention in high school. Some became cheerleaders, some took drugs, and others became dependent on boyfriends. They turned away from academics because they were no longer being rewarded for this type of achievement. Two of the reasons they did not excel were that achievement was no longer based on whether or not they were good girls, and the curriculum started focusing on basic skills and specific content knowledge. In fact, once they started competing with a larger number of students, often they were no longer the best. They turned away from academics because when they were no longer recognized for being the best, they were no longer interested.

Patterns of Achievement in Graduate School

Once the women were able to get past their difficulties in high school and in college, in graduate school they did very well. Their achievement patterns would indicate that they did well in elementary school, less well in high school, better in college and very well in graduate school. Why did the women do well in elementary school and graduate school? These women received more individual attention and recognition in elementary school and in graduate school. Also, in graduate school, students are expected to use higher-level thinking skills. These students could draw on their strengths in reflection and analysis. They started connecting intellectually with the expectations of the schools. In addition, students were allowed to be more independent. Many adult educators claim that returning students (or older students in general) enjoy an andragological style of learning which assumes that adult students are more intrinsically motivated and self-directed (Knowles, 1970; Sheehan, McMenamin & McDevitt, 1992). In many graduate schools, the participants are given responsibility for their own learning and opportunities to explore their own interests.

Pam: How did you like the graduate program there?
Jackie: I loved it. I had a good time. I wouldn't have stayed for a doctorate had I not been having fun—really.
Pam: What was good about the program?
Jackie: What was good about it was I could do exactly what I damned well pleased. I started stopping taking drugs before I went to graduate school, and I absolutely stopped when I was in graduate school, and the reason was because for the first time in my life, I couldn't do what I needed to do and use. Also, graduate school was me-directed. It wasn't somebody telling me to memorize something about a cell membrane that I didn't care about. For the first time, I could do what I wanted to do, and I loved it. So who needs drugs? I was high on grad school.

Joy: This is how the whole thing goes—when I got into graduate school, I thought, now I understand, this is what school is all about. Going through undergrad is paying your dues. When you go to grad school you pick something that interests you and you focus in, you glean from all these cool people and you get all this support. This is grad school! I was so excited.

The women did well in graduate school because they encountered more tolerance for free thinking there than in any other school setting; however, schooling was still not as andragological or as independent as some of the women would have preferred. Even in graduate school, the women's first priority was to make people happy, whether or not they were learning anything. When this happened, the women became frustrated and believed they had to "play the game." This was an adult way to describe what they did as children: learn to read the situation and provide whatever was expected.

Martha: In graduate school, I felt very much like I got a chance to find my own voice, which I still struggle with because I see succeeding in an academic setting as playing the game. There's a part of me that plays the game, that knows how to play the game. I learn what they want, and I do it. Is that male? But then I think of what Carol Gilligan and Mary Belenky have done. They did it. They found a way to be in an academic setting and still open doors for women.

Differences Noted Among the Women of Color

Since there were only a few women of color, I can't make conclusions about differences in achievement patterns as a result of ethnicity. However, I did notice some interesting differences that could be explored by others later. For example, I found that the women of color were more likely to have been involved in special programs. Janus was involved in Upward Bound. Maria and Carmen were involved in gifted programs. Maria was also involved in the Inroads program, which provides mentoring for minority students who are interested in business.

At some time during their education, the women of color all went to highly integrated schools or predominately white schools. All felt comfortable in two cultures. All claimed that color, second language and discrimination never posed a significant barrier for them when they were children. In fact, a few of the women felt resentful that their ethnicity was ignored.

The women of color were much more likely to mention specific people who helped them along the way. They were very grateful for teachers and mentors who provided support, and they were more likely to have had mentors. Along the same lines, the women of color were likely to emphasize the positive aspects of their families and downplay the negative. All credited at least one person in their family as being highly influential (especially mothers).

Finally, another interesting point was that more of the women of color were likely to credit themselves for their achievements. At the end of the interviews, I usually asked the women to describe the one most important reason they succeeded. The women of color often credited themselves or at least one member of their family. The white women rarely credited themselves. Although some credited their mothers, they were also less likely to credit family members.

THOUGHTS ON DEVELOPMENTAL THEORY

This book reinforces many of the theories presented in *Women's Ways of Knowing* (Belenky, et al., 1986), a book that provides a description of women's adult developmental stages. In their book, Belenky and her associates list the following stages of development for women: (1) silence, (2) received knowledge, (3) subjective knowledge, (4) procedural knowledge and (5) constructed knowledge.

I have suggested that women who were disadvantaged as children and succeeded at high levels may have developed slightly differently than the women described by Belenky and her colleagues, especially in relation to the authors' characterization of the subjective knowledge stage which they describe as a passage from passivity to action, from self as static to self as becoming, from silence to a protesting inner voice and infallible gut. In this stage, women start to question authority and rely heavily on their lived expeirences to provide answers. They trust their intuition and seem unwilling to explore alternative explanations. In the authors' description of the subjective knowledge stage they report that a large number of the women in this stage came from "chaotic" backgrounds. The authors make references to the prevalence of sexual abuse among the women they categorize as belonging to subjective knowers. What I found in this project was that my participants seemed to fit into at least two different stages, depending on the topic they were discussing at the time. Sometimes, they could easily have been categorized under the subjective stage which is considered a lower stage of development; at other times they were clearly operating in the constructed knowledge stage which characterizes the highest stage of development. In this stage of development, women attempt to integrate knowledge that they felt intuitively was personally important with knowledge they had learned from others. It makes sense that the women in this book may fall into both categories since they are highly educated and had chaotic backgrounds.

Belenky and her colleagues have made great strides in describing developmental patterns for women. However, I still question whether the complexities associated with class and race are being considered carefully enough when providing descriptions of developmental patterns. As I just mentioned, the women in my study demonstrated patterns of behavior associated with at least two of the development stages described in *Women's Ways of Knowing*. The subjective stage is the lowest of these two. There is an implication that if a woman made a comment that could place her in the subjective stage category, she would be functioning at a lower level of development. I disagree with this argument because when my participants made comments that might place them in the subjective stage, their comments seemed sophisticated and well thought out, but could easily have been misinterpreted as representing a lower level of development. For example, in a chapter that provides a description of the subjective stage, Belenky and her colleagues present an example of a student who rebels against an art professor who provides her with a set of guidelines on how to critique art. The student wanted to critique the art according to her own feelings rather than using a traditional method of critique. Belenky and her colleagues describe this woman as growing out of her subjective stage and into a higher level when she realized that this teacher simply wanted her to learn to communicate in the language of the field. This art student's response to her teacher is similar to the responses of the participants in the current book in comparable situations.

In Belenky and her colleagues' description, it is impossible to evaluate the situation because the authors do not describe the entire context. Did the student understand "tradition" but want to do something different? Did the teacher take time to find out if the student needed to learn this language (maybe she had already been exposed to this information before)? Did he try to understand what type of learning would have been more useful for her at the time? Did he suggest that she include her feelings about the painting and branch out into a more traditional critique from there? Did he suggest that she might try contrasting a "feeling" critique with a more traditional critique while considering how different audiences would respond to each critique? These questions would have made this student think more deeply about the painting and how to critique a painting. Did this young woman really demonstrate a lower level of development when she questioned the validity of this assignment and a higher level of development when she understood the teacher's good intentions? Does understanding the teacher's good intentions demonstrate a higher level of intellectual development, or a higher level of assimilation?

Although Belenky and her colleagues acknowledge the political resistance associated with the student's response, they still present this as an example of a student who was stuck in a subjective stage and unable to see beyond her own feelings. When the art student understood the teacher's good intentions, she went beyond herself and integrated a new perspective. It is reasonable to use this anecdote as an example of a lower stage of development if it does indeed represent development as oppose to resistance. Otherwise, a person is confusing resistance with development and sending messages to nontraditional students that if they resist tradition, they are going to be accused of operating at a lower level of intellectual development.

Some of the women in my book might have rebelled against this art teacher's methods not because they were in a lower level of development, but because they experienced this assignment as an oppressive way of doing things (e.g., male or ethnocentric) that invalidated their methods and their styles. If the women in this book were asked why they were opposed to a traditional critique, they might argue that a guided critique was a structured way to regurgitate the obvious. Most of the women in this book could easily go "beyond themselves" and connect their thinking with the traditional ways of thinking, but many would refuse because they are angry or because they would experience this as mind-numbingly simple, providing little opportunity for originality or voice. Ultimately, my participants were functioning on a higher level of intellectual development but sometimes didn't know how to communicate their ideas (or were afraid to communicate their ideas).

The idea that personal experience and feeling is evidence of a lower level of development is sexist because it is usually considered a "feminine" way of learning and understanding. It is also classist because it is a "lower-class" way of learning. The women in this book were able to go beyond themselves; often they were unwilling. A simple solution to this problem would be for educators to be explicit about what they are trying to accomplish and to allow students who are different to go beyond the traditional methods and incorporate their own style. They should also allow women to integrate personal experience whenever it enhances their learning process. Perhaps what women such as those in this book really need is to be taught how to communicate their novel ideas in ways that traditional people can understand and accept as opposed to being forced to make their ideas conform to traditional models.

So far I have talked about the developmental theories presented in *Women's Ways of Knowing.* In another perspective on adult learning, Gould (1978) describes adult growth as a progressive coming to terms with the emotional realities of what one's life is like as an adult, and hence a shedding of childhood illusions of safety and invincibility. He identifies changing states of consciousness that are age linked. For example, he believes that in our twenties we have the illusion that all will be well if we do "what we are supposed to do," and around thirty, we recognize contradictory inner forces that shred the illusion that life is simple and controllable. At forty we begin to confront death as a real presence and shed the illusion that we will live forever. Gould had his theories grounded in the idea of life stage development as opposed to other theories that do not embed development chronologically in the adult life cycle. In this book, development is not embedded in the idea of life-stage development. However, an interesting question relates to Gould's idea that as an adult, development is based on the idea that childhood illusions of safety and invincibility are shed and adults move on and develop from there. Obviously, this development theory describes children from traditional homes, where safety and security are expected and provided. I suggest that women from disadvantaged backgrounds may develop differently because children from these backgrounds shed the illusion that life is simple and controllable at a very early age. Most children from disadvantaged backgrounds do not feel safe and secure as children. Therefore they need to develop adaptive strategies.

SUMMARY AND CONCLUSIONS

The main argument in this chapter is that resilient girls may develop differently than nonresilient girls or those children who do not face poverty and stress. It is suggested that resilient girls develop a specific type of higher-level thinking ability at an early age. This ability assists them throughout their lives.

Higher-level thinking skills make elementary school easy for such girls. Their success in elementary school plants the idea in their minds that they are smart, and although they have to struggle later in school, they hold on to the idea that they have something special to offer. Unfortunately, their struggles are exacerbated because few people recognize their potential. This oversight is not always the result of blatant discrimination. Educators do not recognize such women's potential because these students often lack basic skills. In addition, although such women have always believed they had something to offer, they can never really describe exactly what that is. Many in this book used the word "empathy," others used the word "intuition," and others claimed they "could fit things together to make a whole." I suggest that the women in this book demonstrated what has recently been described as "emotional intelligence" by

Goleman (1995), "inter- and intrapersonal intelligence" by Gardner (1983) or "critical thinking" by Taylor (1990).

The skills defined in these constructs were overlooked in the past because people have only recently suggested that these skills might characterize a specific type of intelligence. Also, it is possible that since these types of skills were often associated with women, they were never valued in the ways that other types of intelligence were valued. Therefore, it is not surprising that educators have not recognized and encouraged emotional intelligence among students. I am not suggesting that teachers focus only on these strengths. I am suggesting that teachers focus on these strengths as a place to begin building self-esteem, so that ultimately girls can move on and take risks in other areas.

10

FAMILY AND COMMUNITY
INFLUENCES

In other books, authors have focused on how family interactions affect achievement orientation (Clark, 1983; Gandara, 1995). That was not my goal. However, since the women I interviewed were encouraged to discuss any issue they felt was important, it soon became clear that family issues would be included. It is important to emphasize once again that not all of the women in this book had dysfunctional parents. In fact, some of the stressors listed (see Appendix D) related to the death of a parent or to the women's own drug and alcohol use as teenagers. In those families, parents often were considered supportive and played an important role in the participants' achievement process. In fact, even when the women did describe serious problems with family interactions, many still credited at least one member of their family as being highly influential and supportive.

Maria: I still think it all comes back to my mom really. As I get older, I realize what she did by raising three kids on her own with no support from my dad, and going out there with no college education and getting a very good job really. She was the driving force for all of us. One of her biggest goals was to have three daughters who were self-sufficient. She raised very feminist women in her household.

Joy: My dad's a bigot. Actually, he's not anymore. He thought he was, and I had to convince him otherwise. So anyway, when I was growing up, anything he said was automatically wrong, so if he was racist, then I wasn't. If he's conservative, then I'm liberal. Whatever he said, I'd do the opposite. So in the long run, my parents were supportive. I was able to argue with them about being wrong, because they were obviously wrong.

Janus: I think I've always been encouraged. I've always been encouraged by my mother. She's been very important in my life. Not that my father wasn't there, but I was never encouraged by him to the same degree.

Michelle: My confidence probably came from my parents, my dad especially. He had this attitude like, you can do no wrong, you are the center of the universe, unconditional kind of love thing, I felt like whatever I try was fine. I never had any of that —you're not good enough, you can't do this, you're stupid. There was never any of that. And it was balanced by my mother who would always say, "Oh, why don't you do better?" I'd get an A and she'd say, "Well, I knew you could." It seems that she knows what my abilities are and doesn't like crack the whip and say, "Why aren't you doing better." It was always like, "Well, I knew you could." So it's not a surprise.

On the other hand, many of the parents were actively detrimental to their children's achievement. This went beyond an inability to provide guidance and information; some parents were actually quite discouraging and abusive to their children. In these situations, the women continued to achieve despite negative interactions with their parents. They were self-motivated and determined to overcome parent-imposed barriers.

Donna: The situation that I grew up in is that I could spend hours on homework and then my mother would come in and tear it up so that I'd have to go to school without my homework. So it's not that I didn't have the motivation. In fact, I was a perfectionist, but it was just that a lot of times I couldn't follow through. I couldn't for reasons outside of my control.

Martha: I remember that I was shocked when I applied to college. I was known by all my teachers and the career counselor at school. I was one of the top students and I spent a lot of time in the career center exploring different schools and figuring out what I wanted to do, and I had my schools picked out and I applied to top schools in this country, and I got accepted at all of them. And—well—my parents said, "Sorry, you can't go." I was shocked, because I had just assumed that I was going to college.

Shirley: My dad has a chip on his shoulder about his own lack of education, so when I was little I was quite verbal and quite precocious, and looking back I think that anything that I did that demonstrated that precociousness was kind of an affront to him, and my mother didn't want to make waves with him. So when I did something that made him feel a little insecure, this triggered a reaction in him and mostly what he did was squash me. So from that standpoint, anything that I did at school that was an achievement was not anything that he was really very inclined to pay any attention to, and my mother felt like she couldn't. So the things that did happen at school that were positive were very much downplayed in my family.

As the women discussed the role of their family of origin, they were often ambivalent. Some had parents who were extremely helpful; others had parents who were not at all helpful. Most often, however, the family's influence fell somewhere in between these two extremes. In other words, sometimes parents were supportive and sometimes they were not. Sometimes, one parent was supportive and the other was not. Rarely did a women claim that both parents were detrimental in every situation. However, this did happen in a few cases.

Not all of the problems associated with negative parental involvement were as severe as abuse. For example, in many cases the parents had traditional ideas about women and were not supportive of their daughter's professional goals.

Teresa: My mother came from a generation where women did not go to college. She was working-class, middle-class, both, but she was almost embarrassed that I was gifted. I was identified as gifted from the first time I stepped in school. She didn't know what to do with me. Until the day she died, she didn't know what to do with me. She wanted me to be as beautiful as she was, and she wanted me to be a stewardess. That was her aspiration for me.

In other situations, the parents did not understand the benefits of college and wanted their child to do something that could "help her support herself." A few times, parents refused to allow their child to go to college or to go to certain colleges that may have been the most appropriate and beneficial.

Diane: My family was really proud of me after I graduated, but my family is weird. They have a real blue-collar mentality. I worked for Cosco as a cashier as an undergrad, so I just figured that I should keep working there because cashiers can make like $33,000 a year, and even though it's very, very hard work standing up all day, my dad thinks of the money and the security, not what I want to do. That doesn't matter. To them, happiness doesn't matter. None of these things matter. They don't understand. Ultimately I know that they're proud of me, but now they think that I'm going too far with this thing, they always ask, "When are you ever going to get a real job?"

Toni: My family thinks I'm insane. I've been in graduate school for eight years. To them it's almost like I've been in a mental institution for eight years.
Pam: They don't really understand?
Toni: They think it's so weird. They think it's so bizarre. They'll say stuff like, "Well she's smart. She could have done something that would help her earn a living." I guess they don't think a Ph.D. in biology will get me a job.

Michelle: I was definitely the first one to go to college, and not only did I go to college, I kept going to college. My family thinks I'm nuts. They're looking at me like, "When do you get a real job?"

Debbie: My family insisted that I go to college but demeaned my education by saying things like, "You've got too much education," and calling me a "know-it-all."

NEW PERSPECTIVE ON PARENT INVOLVEMENT

In general, educators believe that parents should always be involved in their child's educational process. When parents are not involved, the school will try to increase parent participation. It is interesting then, that many of these women believed that they succeeded because they were able to create a separation between school and home.

Teresa: School was my rescue. I knew then that I was escaping. It was my way out. I knew it. By the time I was 11, I knew. My mother was a full alcoholic and addicted to prescription pills and a socialite. She was a mean drunk. She was not a nice drunk. I wanted out dreadfully by that time. Very much so.

Shirley: To some extent, the things that I went through when I was a kid were distracting, but on the other hand, a lot of the things that I did in school were a relief, and provided kind of a refuge from what was going on in my life, and there's something very nicely mind numbing about working math problems.

June: I liked school in sixth grade because it was more stable. That's what really comes to me about school is that school was stable for me. And I looked for that stability.

Toni: In some ways, school felt like a safe place? It was organized and structured and I think I liked that. I really liked that.

Martha: We were in danger if we didn't keep the house clean. That was serious. That was why school was safe—because you could do stuff at school and not get in trouble for it, but at home, you never knew what was going to be wrong. That was the other thing about my mom—you just never knew what you would do that would upset her. It might be that you didn't make your bed right, or it might be that you were making too much noise, and all of a sudden—and that was true for my dad too. If you made too much noise, he would get violently angry, and that was really scary.

Maria: To me, school was the place away from all the bad things that were happening at home. There I could be really, really good. I think partly (and now I'm not sure that a seven-year-old child knows this consciously) that if I did really, really well there, maybe the bad things would go away at home. It was one place where I could be really good and everything would happen really well and nothing would go wrong.

The women I interviewed did well on their own as children and school was a sanctuary away from home, a place where they could be successful. Since many of the women were using school to help them disassociate from the dysfunction at home, the result was often negative when their families did intrude upon their life at school.

Pam: Did you tell anybody about your disadvantage?

Janet: No, I never told anybody. I think I might have stood out initially for my grades, but then once they knew who I was, if they started listening to gossip— There were times, like at the health club changing clothes, I'd hear gossip about my parents.

June: School was this really secure place and I could be a different person at school than I was at home. I could be this really highly functional person at the school. But then when it did spill over, because there was times where that was uncontrollable, it encouraged me even more to be secretive and to not feel good about myself because anytime I did have that spill over, like in the situation where I couldn't keep my image together, I got negative reactions.

Sara: I probably would have been mortified if a teacher had said, "You seem really depressed." I've read a lot of stuff about dysfunctional families and the way they cover up what goes on at home. Certainly, I never did that consciously, but I wonder to what extent that was part of it. I was being the best kid in the school so that people wouldn't know that my dad came home drunk every night. It's kind of interesting because I wonder what I'd do now, knowing about the way Catholic parishes work, everybody covers up equally problematic family situations.

Donna was the only woman who claimed there was little or no separation between home and school. She found this to be highly distracting, and was therefore less positive about elementary school than the other participants. She claimed that she was constantly stressed because teachers knew about her family situation.

I am not suggesting that educators should encourage children to hide who they are and discourage parental contact with the school, but rather that school officials should learn how to use such information more effectively. In Donna's case, the nuns often would empathize with her mother when she told them untrue stories about her daughter's bad behavior. Once a nun asked Donna why she was such a bad child. At other times, the nuns believed Donna and felt sorry for her. In other words, it wasn't parental contact per se that negatively affected this woman, it was the dysfunctional way the school officials reacted to the situation. Ultimately, the principal of this school positively affected Donna's life, when she changed her low grades to straight A's so she could get accepted into a private boarding school. So ultimately it was better that the principal knew Donna's situation and took a proactive stance in changing her life.

In some cases, school or societal interventions that are detrimental may be worse than no intervention at all. It was interesting that all of the women in this book lived throughout most of the childhood with both parents. Those who did not live with both parents, lived with one parent. None were ever placed in foster homes, temporary living arrangements, drug rehabilitation facilities or orphanages. They tried to avoid their family's dysfunction and most often they avoided our society's dysfunctional system of assistance. Ultimately, they avoided both systems. The problems associated with parental involvement remind us that certain interventions (even very popular ones) will not work with all kids. We cannot assume that all interventions work the same way for all kids in every situation.

RELATIONSHIP WITH SIBLINGS

In a family unit, a child's relationship with his or her siblings is important. People talk about the culture of dysfunction, but that culture is never completely defined. Siblings were part of the culture that surrounded the women who volunteered for my project. Although children sometimes bond when they face stress, other times they turn against each other. In the interviews, women talked about both the positive and negative influence of their siblings. Helen believed that one of her older sisters actually saved her education when she was young by providing lunch money.

Helen: My mother thought that if you didn't have enough money to pay for a child's lunch, then you shouldn't send that child to school. It was screwy reasoning, but that was one of the reasons that I felt that I had been lucky—that I was able to stay in school. First, my sister had stood up for me and recognized how important it was to me and sent money every week so that I could have lunch.

Although a number of the participants' siblings did very well, a larger number of siblings did not do well. Family functioning has an enormous impact on children, but this variable should not be studied in isolation. Although the women in this book are now productive members of the community, many of their siblings are not. In fact, in two cases, the women had siblings who committed suicide, many other siblings were involved with drugs and a large number never graduated from high school.

Sara: One of my sisters, unfortunately, died. She committed suicide when she was 21. She got into drugs fairly young, 15 maybe, ran away from home, had a child by a guy who was a heroin dealer. She killed herself when she was 21, leaving a three-year-old child, which was extremely sad. The child was then given into the custody of its dad, who was the heroin dealer. He got killed, murdered actually, in a drug deal when the kid was 12. Then the kid went to live with his grandfather, who was not a great parent, but wanted to make up for the failure with his son. He managed to alienate the grandson. This kid is now 21 and clearly has lots of problems. Right now he's with a group of fundamentalist, born-again Christians, but before that he was into Satanism, and before that, he was into drugs. Who knows where this one's going to go next?

June: My brother is not in trouble as far as jail. He's got a business, but he's 20 years old and he has a baby. The baby is a year old and the mother of the baby is 17 years old, and so far the parents are not married. So I see him as repeating that cycle. Also, the mother of my nephew told me the other day that she needed money from my brother for the baby's first birthday and he wouldn't give her the money because he was spending all his money on drinking.

Even when their siblings did well, many of the women still did not have a positive relationship with them. Parents often compared their children and set up a dynamic of competition between them. Since the women in this book were always successful, their parents often compared their academic progress with that of their siblings, causing the siblings to resent them. This was an added stress.

June: Another thing, I really felt like my parents put a big division between my brother and I because they were constantly holding me up to him, saying, "June's doing this and why can't you do this?" It put a lot of distance between us and made it hard for us to have a relationship.

Sara: I know now from talking to my sisters and brothers that they really resented being compared with me at school, and the nuns were not very knowledgeable about educational theory. Their way of motivating children was, "Why can't you be like your big sister?" And so consequently, my sisters and brothers rebelled in school because of the messages they were getting.

Martha: In junior high school, I was tormented by a group of kids constantly. I'd take the bus home from school and they'd wait and hide and beat me up and torment me. I felt like it was because I was slow and fat and they made friends with my little sister, and my little sister hated me. She hated me. She was really, really angry, and I think she still hates me. At home, I not only had to try not to make my parents mad, I had to try not to make her mad, too. And we're very competitive. It was something my parents almost encouraged. All four of us were really competitive. They just didn't equal things out. They didn't know how to appreciate what each of us could do well, so we would all try to out do each other, and that was kind of hard.

HOW STRESS AFFECTS ACHIEVEMENT

A recent criticism of people (like myself) who study the special needs of people from disadvantaged backgrounds is that we almost exclusively concentrate on the poor. Since family functioning can be a significant barrier, many middle- and upper-class children also face stress. Of course, being poor can be a major stress in and of itself, and people who are poor are more likely to face other kinds of stresses. That is why poorness is such a common theme in a book like this one. Still, I felt that stressful life events posed the most significant barrier for these women I found the greatest differences between those who had less stress as children and those who had more stress as children. The ones who were most positive and achieved earlier were those who had supportive parents. The ones who were most negative and achieved later in life were those who had dealt with greater stress as children and young adults.

I have come to the conclusion that the stress these women faced affected many aspects of their achievement process, but mostly it made them more fearful. They were afraid to talk in front of people; they were afraid to seek help from professors; they were afraid to apply to prestigious graduate schools.

Their fears made them vulnerable to criticism, and it made them choose majors where they were less likely to receive negative feedback. I believe we all have fears, whether or not we were disadvantaged as children. However, I also believe that women who faced stress as children are often more fearful than those who were taught to have faith in their abilities. It is my guess that boys and girls are different. It is possible that when faced with stress as children, boys become angry and girls become fearful, and beyond that, boys become violent and girls withdraw.

June: Because of experiences with my father, I think I've been more intimidated by male teachers. It's harder for me to interact with males that are in an authority position. My father was not a consistent figure for me. He was unpredictable. He drank. He was the boss. He was in control, and everything centered around him and his needs. He was a very threatening figure. He'd raise his voice and throw things when he got mad, and he really scared me. And he abused me. He abused me sexually. So of course, he really scared me.

Pam: Why were you shy?
Toni: I think it's insecurity. I think it's an old pattern, a survival pattern in my family. It's like, observe from the corner. Don't ask any questions or you're going to get hit.

Janet: I think that it took a lot more for me to concentrate than it did for other students because I was only using about 20 percent of my mind for school. More of it was spent on the mental energy of, "God, what's mom going to be like when I get home? "or "what if she called one of my friend's moms and did something weird?"—that sort of worrying.

IMMEDIATE FAMILY

In the next few sections, I explain how the extended family, the immediate family and the community influenced the women's achievement. Some may wonder if these women achieved because they married wealthy men or lived with a wealthy partner who paid their way through college. The answer is no! Only two women out of 21 claimed that their husbands financially supported them through school, and this was only during their master's programs. These same two women had supported themselves as undergraduates. Many of the women (12 out of 21) were single. Eleven of these women had never been married. A few other women, however, emphasized that their husbands (or significant others) were emotionally supportive throughout their educational process.

Shirley: So my husband is terrific, and he just got laid off at a company that closed the plant, and so he got six months' worth of severance pay. So we've been using that to live on because he hasn't found a job up here. When we go to Boston, he's going to look for a job. So in other words, it wasn't too bad getting through graduate school because we have existing employment, but now it is really hard. Doing this postdoctoral training kind of thing where you have to go around the country would be impossible if I had kids or we had income restrictions. But we're spending our savings on this, so it better work out. That's right. That's the fear, at the end of this, I've got to get a job somewhere.

Maria: When I had to make a decision about graduate school, it helped that my husband is really supportive of everything that I do. So, you know, I'd say, "Well, what do you think?" And he'd say, "Just go for it. Just do it. You can do it, you know; you can!"

Most often, unfortunately, the partners in these women's lives were detrimental. A few times, the women supported their husbands through school, causing a delay in their progress. At other times, they were involved in abusive relationships or had to handle a traumatic divorce during important stages of their schooling.

Donna: That was a big mistake [marriage] because he was really bad news. He was a really bad choice. And it really hurt my career, or the career that I was on, the path that I was on—really, really, really hurt it badly.

In these situations, their relationships added stress to their lives and made it difficult for them to concentrate on their schoolwork. Also, all of the women who went through a divorce became responsible for their children and had to adapt to a single-parent lifestyle. The point is, only a few of the women got any type of support from their husbands (or significant others), and none of the women credited their husbands for their success as a result of financial or intellectual support. Actually, many mentioned their significant others only in passing.

As for children, the results were mixed. A few of the women claimed that the reason they achieved highly was because they wanted something better for their children.

Pam: If you could name one reason why you achieved—?
Janus: Now that's going to be my daughter. I think I have to succeed for her, because it's going to impact very heavily on her. I think it all boils down to being able to make sure that somebody else can come along—and my daughter is all I have. I don't want her to have to carry the torch or anything like that, but you just hope that in some way it'll impact on her and she'll be encouraged by it, and she'll believe in herself more as an individual, as a young black woman. And she'll be stronger for it in some ways. And maybe take a little bit of it with her into her life.

However, all the women who were mothers described the difficulties of taking classes while caring for small children. These mothers would not describe their children as a barrier, but they did emphasize the difficulties associated with being a parent and going to school. They felt that men and women who are not parents do not understand and acknowledge the difficulties associated with combining parenting and achievement.

Donna: I'm really devoted to my kids, and it's been really hard for me to be a doctoral student, and I always go back and forth about can I complete this, because to be a "scholar," quote, unquote, I mean, you really have to invest yourself totally in your work, and I can't do it. My daughter just hit adolescence and it's really tough, so I'm constantly thinking, "Can I really pull this off?" This has been the hardest part of my whole academic career. Before, things were really easy for me. I could sit in a class and ace a test. Now I really need time to think, to conceptualize and do a lot of different types of cognitive activity. I just don't have the time to do it.

COMMUNITY AND EXTENDED FAMILY

A few of the women described the positive influence of their community. In this book, I define community as a person's friends, neighbors, colleagues, extended family and organizations like the Girl Scouts. Community influences were not a major issue with every participant. Yet enough people described community assistance to make it worth mentioning. Those who emphasized the influences of community complained that families have become too isolated. A few of the women suggested that it was more difficult for stressed families to connect with others. In a few of the dialog quotes listed below, it is obvious that some women were helped enormously by people outside their family of origin.

Janus: I think I was blessed. I think I was lucky that I had parents and friends and family and people in my life that seemed to really care about what happened to my life. Every time I go home, I make sure that I see all those people to let them know that I'm still doing okay.

Joy: I was a Girl Scout. I don't know if that has anything to do with my resiliency, but I was a Girl Scout all the way through high school right up to the end. I had the best Girl Scout leader on the face of the earth. We did all sorts of cool, wonderful educational things that seemed like fun. I would go to Girl Scouts, and then the leader would drive me to the hospital to see my dad. Everybody around me—my mother's friends, my Girl Scout leader, the bus driver, all knew about my family situation and helped us.

Jennifer: The thing that was good in my neighborhood too was that some of the parents in the neighborhood—they really had a certain sense of respect for me, and they wished that their kids would be like me. Not because I was like some Goody Two -shoes, but because I was good in school.

June: Having my grandparents living with us helped me a lot. They took care of me all of the time, and they were really a big resource for me, having them so accessible.

Janet: My aunt and uncle helped me a lot. A couple of times in graduate school when I didn't have money, they would just somehow (manna from heaven), send me fifty bucks, a hundred bucks, enough so that I could have food. One Christmas they sent me a plane ticket, which was the biggest gift anybody had ever given me, and I was like, wow, a plane ticket, so I could have the holiday with them in a normal, tranquil home situation. I didn't have to think about who was going to fight with whom. Those kindnesses at the right moment can really make all the difference.

Teresa: My very best friend was the valedictorian and I was the salutatorian, and we were college roommates and we became engaged to college roommates. She died right after college. She died right after childbirth. She was my real thing. Her family again recognized immediately what my parents were, and they took me in. They were simple tobacco farm people, and Donna was gifted and I was gifted. They were my second home. In fact, I lived there for most of my senior year.

Anne: I had a very best friend and we banded together. She was doing actually very well in school in the things she liked to do. She was wild also, so we were very good friends and shared everything.

Teresa: I had really good friends in my spiritual communities who were there for me, and I was real good about seeking out and getting help.

SUMMARY AND DISCUSSION

I was surprised that even those participants who faced an enormous amount of childhood stress described at least one member of their family as influential. In fact, many participants listed family members (especially mothers) as the one factor in their lives that was most important in helping them achieve. Furthermore, family members, even more than education professionals, encouraged the women in this book.

Although many of the women did credit family members for helping them, most of them wanted a separation between home and school. They experienced school as a safe and pleasant place away from the chaos in their homes. The hesitancy the women felt about integrating home and school was most often associated with their fear that the school would not respond appropriately to their personal disclosure or to their parents' involvement.

Although the women did talk extensively about their families of origin, most of the women did not talk about their immediate families. When they did speak about significant others, usually they described them as helpful and encouraging. However, some were not, especially when a woman had gone through a traumatic divorce. None of the women credited their husbands, boyfriends or significant others for their achievement. However, many women claimed that their children motivated them to continue because they wanted to provide something "better" for them.

Women also mentioned the importance of the community. Although their experiences were most affected by their family of origin, their extended family, and their friends and neighbors were also helpful at important times during their achievement process.

11

WHY DO SOME WOMEN SUCCEED?

In the previous chapters, I have talked about specific aspects of the women's experience. After considering these experiences, you may still wish to hear an overarching explanation of why these women achieved despite their barriers. How could they achieve so highly when achievement is difficult even for those who face fewer barriers? Rhodes and Brown (1991) wrap up their book on resiliency by stating that

the how and why of resiliency result from a mixture of the life experiences that children have to choose from. Some children are insulated by positive family experiences; others are not. Some children are protected by strong personal characteristics; others are not. Some children are bolstered by intervening environmental circumstances; others are not. Within this scenario the child makes decisions (both consciously and subconsciously) predicated upon an evaluation of past, ongoing, and current life experiences in the above mentioned areas. (p. 174)

I agree with this summary statement. Unfortunately, it leaves us in the dark because it suggests that resiliency is affected by a million different "obstacles," over most of which we have no control. Resiliency is a role of the dice, a spin of the wheel. As a child, did you get one of the "good" things that will help you compensate (a mentor, a supportive mother, a good teacher)? Will your stubborn personality make up for your family dysfunction? Are you attractive and outgoing?

Of course resiliency is more or less likely depending on various influences, but we don't have to rely on chance. There are some identifiable personality traits and school interventions that can help us predict and encourage resiliency.

In this book, I have uncovered some common characteristics and experiences that led the women down a similar path toward achievement. Each woman had her own unique experience; still, most were surprised to find that so many other women had similar feelings and experiences.

No Identification: I was very impressed with how similar my experiences and attitudes were to the other participants in the study, both in terms of the interpretations and the quoted passages.

ELEMENTARY SCHOOL

It was clear that in elementary school, all of the women were given reinforcement for being smart and special. They were well liked by their teachers and considered good girls. School became a safe and pleasant place where they were reinforced for effort and ability. At their homes, the atmosphere was often chaotic and inconsistent. School was a place where they could be successful.

The women did well in elementary school for many reasons. Most were "nice girls" and were reinforced for good behavior. These girls demonstrated behavior that was attractive to teachers because at an early age they developed what has been described as a high level of emotional intelligence. This type of intelligence not only assisted them to behave in ways that pleased the teacher, it is a type of intelligence that allows children to think on a higher level about many different topics. The children were good in school because they were "smart." They were intellectually superior, especially in certain areas that rely on, or draw from, personal intelligence.

HIGH SCHOOL

In high school the women did less well but continued to seek out information that led them down the path of success. They never gave up the idea that they wanted to go to college, and even if they didn't start college right after high school, as they worked, they continued to seek opportunities to go back. One way they maintained their reputations for being good students in high school was to choose classes where they could continue to earn good grades. Although some people would call these classes "easier," for these women the classes were easier because they tapped into the talents they had developed in the lower grades related to personal intelligence.

It is also important to point out that in high school most of the women avoided the trap of falling in love with the wrong boy and settling down early with children and a family. As a teenager Janus did give birth to a child, and a few of the women did marry young, but many were later divorced, and those who stayed married continued to achieve in spite of the difficulties of juggling family responsibilities.

COLLEGE

There was no one way that students got into college. As undergraduates, many of the women went to junior colleges, state schools or private liberal arts colleges. Only a couple were accepted at the most prestigious private schools. For the most part, they went to inexpensive junior colleges or state schools and were able to pay their own way by obtaining financial aid and working. Most of the women had above-average grades and decent test scores as high school students. And most didn't really care what university they attended as undergraduates. For these women, going to college at all was an incredible triumph, regardless of which school they attended. Many only applied to one university.

As undergraduate students, the women usually felt they were jumping through hoops to obtain diplomas, not developing any intellectual skills. They still had no guidance and often applied to the wrong colleges, started and stopped their education at different universities, and majored in the wrong areas. In many cases the women earned more than one degree or major. For example, after Brandy completed an art degree as an undergraduate, she had to go back to earn another two-year degree focusing on math in order for her to apply to graduate programs in architecture. Those who went to small private colleges as undergraduates had the most help and the best experiences.

GRADUATE SCHOOL

Many more of the women went to prestigious universities as graduate students. By the time they applied for graduate school, they learned that different universities were more or less prestigious. Their self-confidence had also grown to the point that they believed they should at least apply to better schools. Still, most were surprised (almost shocked) when they were admitted into these prestigious schools.

The reasons women got into better schools as graduate students were as varied as the ways they paid for their education. Some had special jobs that helped them. For example, before applying to graduate school, Joy had a job in the Peace Corps and worked at a very impressive job in an African country. Even those who did not have "special jobs" usually had some full-time work experience and were able to get good recommendations from former employers. A few did attend prestigious schools as undergraduates, which is helpful. All had earned good grades in college and most had test scores that were average or above-average for students in their fields. Some took extra classes from different universities after their undergraduate degrees to prepare for them graduate work. Although it was rare, a few had mentors who provided guidance.

Some had special ways to get money, through either social security, scholarships, work or financial aid. As mentioned earlier, however, most spent some time in state-supported schools rather than at expensive private schools.

The women received more support and encouragement in graduate school. Also, they did fairly well academically because they connected intellectually with the culture of graduate school, where professors often focus on theory, personal experience, and higher-level thinking.

Although the women had better experiences in graduate school than in college or high school, it was still difficult. The women suffered from the impostor complex, which made them afraid to speak out, to take risks and to explore areas such as math and technology. Ultimately, however, they tried and were surprised that their accomplishments actually propelled them forward. They conquered their fears and did well, but often did not enjoy the process.

CAREERS

I mentioned in previous chapters that some women from disadvantaged backgrounds feel uncomfortable as they move into higher-level positions at work. In fact, successful women in higher-level positions often believe they must hide the negative (or unusual) aspects of their histories, feel isolated and different, and question whether their difficulties result from difference or lack of talent.

People are often made to feel uninformed when they don't know (or are unwilling to participate in) the elitist language of certain groups. Many have suffered consequences for taking a moral stance against those in power. Some feel like outsiders who must hide their true identities and became what others expect. The women in this book found that an important part of the achievement process was recognizing that they had to fight for their own identity, and some people even appreciated what they had to offer. Women need to trust their instincts and be firm in their decisions. They need to find their voice and speak their minds. Unfortunately, women in higher-level positions often learn these lessons very slowly and in ways that cause stress and emotional pain. They learn, and they continue, but the process is not pleasant. They keep hoping to reach that place: acceptance into a program (medical, Ph.D., law), a tenure-track faculty position, a perfectly managed project, that well-produced movie, any accomplishment that will give them power to stop questioning themselves and start enjoying the process. Unfortunately, this doesn't happen early in most women's careers. Sometimes it happens late, and sometimes the defining moment never arrives.

SUMMARY AND DISCUSSION

I am not the only person who has sought to understand why some women achieve highly despite barriers. In this area, most authors have solicited input from successful women in minority groups or in particular occupations (Flores, 1988; Furumoto, 1980; Gotwalt & Towns, 1986; Hobson-Smith, 1982; O'Connell & Russo, 1980; Smith, 1982; Wyche & Graves, 1992). For example, Hobson-Smith (1982) interviewed 12 African-American women who have achieved highly in academics and who also worked in higher education. The profiles in that article indicate that these women became aware of their potential in their formative years. Each was nurtured and encouraged by strong family members and occasionally by professionals, such as teachers. These high-achieving African-American women possessed a keen awareness of their strengths and a commitment to better the lives of all people, especially African Americans. The majority of them felt they had been victims of both race and sex discrimination and had to exert energy to fight both. They believed this wasted their time, which could have been better utilized doing other things. They firmly believed that hard work and preparation were the essential ingredients for career success.

In another example, Gotwalt and Towns (1986) surveyed 176 women school superintendents (of which 24 were also interviewed). In that project:

• 90 percent were firstborn children in the family.
• 90 percent grew up in rural communities.
• 75 percent were reared within 200 miles of where they now work.
• Most had supportive families.
• Most had parents who placed a high priority on education.
• Most had parents who held high expectations.
• Most experienced sibling rivalry often.
• Most had either female teachers or their mothers as role models.
• Most fathers were considered a strong support.
• 95 percent participated extensively in school, community and church activities.
• Most were in student councils, debate teams and honor societies.
• Most claimed that their greatest career support (later) came from husbands and children.

Obviously, however, the findings in Gotwalt and Town's (1986) study indicate that these women were not raised in stressful environments. Quite to the contrary, it seems most of these women were raised in very supportive environments.

While some research has explored the needs of minority women, very little research has focused on women who have faced other disadvantages beyond those associated with minority status. Specifically, few researchers have attempted to understand and describe the special needs of women who have faced multiple disadvantages, especially those who experienced traumatic stress as children.

Harrington and Boardman conducted a study that used biographical information to explain why some people from disadvantaged backgrounds achieve (in Wells, 1989). These investigators interviewed 30 men (15 white and 15 black) and 30 women (15 white and 15 black) whom they described as people who were disadvantaged as children and were now successful as adults. Subjects were considered disadvantaged if their parents did not graduate from high school or if their parents had low-status jobs. These investigators also interviewed 40 people whom they described as not being disadvantaged. Subjects were not disadvantaged if at least one of their parents had graduated from high school or held a higher-status job. According to their findings, men and women who were successful despite disadvantage

• were willing to confront obstacles directly rather than indirectly
• were more likely to turn failure around to their advantage
• were better trained for failure
• had an internal locus of control
• were self-sufficient
• were strongly motivated to achieve
• were reward oriented

Some of their conclusions are similar to mine even though Harrington and Boardman's project (in Wells, 1989) is different from mine in many ways. Most important, their definition of disadvantage is very different. In fact, I would argue that their definition is incomplete. Although parent education level has been recognized as an important achievement factor, it is not the only source of disadvantage. Although many of the women in the this book were poor as children, part of a minority group, first-generation college students and mistreated as children, most had at least one parent who graduated from high school. If these same women had participated in Harrington and Boardman's study, they would have been considered advantaged. Furthermore, these researchers seem vague about their definition of success. In their study, people were successful if they had high occupational status (upper-middle class or professional class) in business, academia, or government.

Finally, in another study, Patricia Gandara (1982) interviewed 17 Mexican-American women who were from lower socioeconomic backgrounds and who also succeeded in completing a J.D., M.D., or Ph.D. degree. Although the author did not focus on her participants' childhood stress, they could easily be labeled disadvantaged not only because of their race and economic status, but also because they were first generation (in this country) and most of their families spoke only Spanish in the home. In her study, Gandara emphasized family influences. Specifically, her findings showed that a mother's encouragement to persist, a strong work ethic in the family, a nonauthoritarian style of parenting, and equal treatment for girls and boys were all important factors in promoting success. Although it was reported that a large percentage of these women lived in homes where they spoke Spanish, the women also attributed some of their success to the fact that they were comfortable with both Hispanic and Anglo culture. The investigator credited their comfort to the fact that most of these women had attended highly integrated schools. Finally, one last relevant finding was that the women in Gandara's study most often credited their successes to their families, while men most often attribute their success to inner strength. This was also a characteristic of the women who were interviewed for this book. They often blamed themselves for their failures and credited their families with their successes.

So why did the women in this book achieve? First, whether positive or negative, they adapted and assimilated to the majority culture. They hid who they were because they believed their backgrounds reflected on them negatively. Their circumstances at home motivated them to seek out reinforcement in other places, and they sought reinforcement in the only way they knew how, by being good girls and excelling in school. Since most girls develop faster in elementary school than boys, elementary school was easy for them. This was especially true for this group, since they acquired higher-level thinking skills early to protect themselves from childhood stress. Later, in high school, academics were not as easy, because in elementary school these girls had concentrated on gaining reinforcement through behaviors rather than through learning. Still, since these women were convinced in elementary school that they were smart and special, they never gave up the idea that they had something special to offer. And although it was difficult, they adjusted in high school and especially in college to the amount of effort needed to compensate for the changes in expectations. As adults, they continued to attract some attention and some rewards for their accomplishments, so their belief that they could earn rewards (money, status, etc.) continued to motivate them on their difficult journey. Their motivation was enhanced by the fact that they were drawn toward something (e.g., graduate school, positions at work, etc.) where they could use their intellectual abilities. They were never satisfied with jobs that did not challenge their intellect. Although these women achieved highly, the process of being educated was not always enjoyable, because often they lacked confidence, felt out of place, and clashed with an educational system that is often still more suited to traditional students. Still, these women persevered because they were motivated to change their lives and prove they were capable.

12

TRANSFORMING EDUCATION

It seems useless to talk about the idealistic ways that we "should" change education without thinking about the challenges we face when making these changes. So many times, I have read the final chapter of a book similar to this one where the author writes a wonderfully inspirational essay about how we can all work together to transform education while standing on our heads. By the time I finish reading, I'm left wondering if the author has ever taught in a classroom, worked at a school, attended a faculty meeting or performed gymnastics.

I do believe, however, that it is possible to make changes in education that would meet most of the idealistic challenges that the women in this book pose to education professionals. My idealism was renewed when I started working at the Institute for Educational Transformation (IET) at George Mason University in Virginia Although I would like to take credit for helping to develop this program, I've worked there only a short time. Still, I was so impressed with this professional development program for teachers that later in the chapter, I will use it as an example of what people can accomplish when they dedicate themselves to making positive change.

First, however, I would like to address some of the difficulties associated with implementing changes in education. After carefully reflecting on what the women in this book said they needed and wanted from schools, I have chosen to discuss the difficulties associated with three aspects of what the women said they needed. First, they wanted teachers to know and care about them, and second, they wanted teachers to understand and value differences. Third, they wanted to diminish arrogance and elitism in schools, (as well as the restrictive atmosphere) that often results from an entrenched hierarchical structure.

KNOWING AND CARING FOR STUDENTS

Suggesting that teachers should know each of the children they teach as individuals is a wonderful yet idealistic solution to many school problems. Ferree (1985) provides an interesting discussion about the realities of "knowing how students feel." He describes the ambiguity of defining this phrase and questions whether we should strive to know how students feel, given the difficulty of getting to know children in our current educational structure. Then, at the end of his article, rather than concluding that this is an impossible task, he suggests that one way to teach preservice teachers how to "know students" is to instruct them in what he calls "empathic cognition."

For teachers to have known the women in this book, they would have needed to be experts in empathic cognition. The women actively hid who they were throughout most of their schooling. They wanted teachers to magically know them without needing to disclose information about their personal lives, and they wanted teachers to know how to teach them despite their barriers. Debbie talks of this desire.

Debbie: I've never thought about this before, so I can't think what it would have been like to have somebody who wasn't there to heal me, who was just there to understand who I was and make me learn despite it. I think that would have been a good deal. Not like, "Oh I'm going to take care of you. I want to fix you, or your emotional problems"—but just somebody who got it. Someone who understood what I was going through and who imposed learning anyway. That would have been cool.

Although the women actively hid who they were, this is not the time to fault the survivor. Hiding their backgrounds helped these women to succeed, and it is common practice to hide negative personal experience. In the past, I have explored how students talk about themselves in college courses. Once, in an urban education class where the topics focused on how to educate minority and disadvantaged students, I sought to understand how people talked about their personal experience as minority students, disadvantaged students and as professionals (LePage, 1991). Although it was perfectly appropriate (and encouraged) for students to bring in examples from their own experiences, rarely did any of the college students talk about themselves as minority or disadvantaged students. Instead, they talked about themselves as professionals. After presenting a questionnaire to this class, I was shocked to find that 70 percent of the students considered themselves either a member of a minority group, from a disadvantaged background, or both. The norms surrounding self-disclosure and the attitudes toward unusual personal histories are changing. This leaves people unsure when it is appropriate to disclose information. It is safer to say nothing about your background than to risk acquiring a reputation that you are strange or too emotional. The question is, how can teachers know students when it is still inappropriate for students to disclose personal information about themselves? Joy talks about her discomfort with disclosing information:

Joy: In an ideal world, I would want to have a close relationship with a teacher, one where we would know about each other. But that's not the way this educational system is set up. There's still that power differential, and as long as there's still a power differential, then I don't want Professor X to know everything about me, but I do really want the experience of Professor X knowing everything about me.

In this particular quote, Joy highlights an issue that has been underemphasized in the past, and has recently been brought to the forefront in educational discussions. This is the idea that teachers need to understand the complex relationships that develop between them and their students (Hollingsworth, 1994; Noddings, 1992; Sockett, 1993). Noddings emphasizes the importance of caring. Sockett emphasizes the role of moral decision making. Both believe relationships are important. The women in this book talk about how they want teachers and mentors to know them, understand them, care about them and provide positive reinforcement without coming across as superior or aloof. It is possible to observe how Joy's relationship with her junior high school teacher had a significant effect on her feelings about curriculum and pedagogy. She is interested in the content, and she is happy to be discussing a topic that is intellectually challenging, yet her relationship with the teacher is having a significant impact on this particular learning episode.

Joy: In my junior high school, all the teachers went on a first-name basis. There was an air of respect, an understanding that students had something to offer. I was Joy and he was Russell, and you're Pam, and we're talking about world religion and he's offering his opinion of Hinduism and I'm pointing out what's wrong with Catholicism, and we're comparing it with Kant's sixties impressions. It was a real-life discussion and it was interesting, as opposed to worksheets.

To know students and care about students is difficult. Organizational structures are not in place to reinforce the development of caring relationships. Teachers are not being taught empathic cognition, and they are not given the time to reflect on the complex relationships they develop with their students. Most do not have time to discuss pedagogy and curriculum with their colleagues, let alone reflect on specific relationship issues. The point is, time is not provided, and the rewards are not in place for developing caring relationships.

Pam: Were you hired as a professor because you cared about students?
Janus: Oh, no, no, no—no, no, no, I wasn't hired for that. I think I might have been hired because I was genuine, because I came across as being somebody who was honest and trustworthy and maybe caring to some degree. But—no, that wasn't it. I don't think that was the reason they hired me.

Knowing and caring about students as individuals is important because providing educational support goes beyond awareness of barriers confronting certain groups. Some would go as far as to argue that people should not be grouped according to common characteristics (eg., ethnicity or disadvantage) because it robs people of their individuality. However, the reality is that some outcomes are more or less likely depending on whether people can be identified with certain groups. Yet this book illustrates that group membership does not reliably explain or predict positive and negative outcomes. I found that although many of the women in this book had faced similar barriers, each barrier impeded learning and achievement in different ways depending on the individual. So individuals were affected by similar barriers in dissimilar ways. Also, some of the barriers listed by the participants (e.g., expectations for women) could also affect students who might be labeled privileged. Obviously we should be aware of educational concerns that are more or less likely due to group membership, and we should also strive to understand individual response to barriers.

One way to start recognizing individual responses to barriers is to distinguish between different types of barriers. There are at least two type of barriers. One type is associated with concrete needs. For example, if students need money for college, we should provide financial support. If they need to speak English, we should teach them English. If they are in a wheelchair and cannot walk up three flights of stairs, we should install an elevator. The second type of barrier is psychological. In other words, if a disabled student does not have access to the third floor, this could cause more than just a momentary delay; it could affect a student's sense of belonging, independence and self-confidence. In this framework, understanding the thickness of the barrier (how deeply each barrier affects individual students) is just as important as knowing what barriers exist. For example, in this book the women were more or less affected by race-related issues depending on where they lived as children, their family's response to race and their own experience with racism. It seems likely that people who face multiple barriers, including women and nontraditional students, do not always reach their potential because educators do not address the first layer of barriers, let alone the second, effectively. Furthermore, educators do not know students well enough to understand how each barrier affects them individually.

In the past, many special education students have suffered from being labeled. However, rather than responding to this problem by pretending that everyone is the same, a better solution is to understand and label barriers (as opposed to labeling the person). Also, it is important to discard the negative connotations associated with labels. The women in this book didn't mind having their barriers labeled; they were happy that their difficulties were being acknowledged and that they were finally being recognized for moving beyond their barriers.

UNDERSTANDING AND ACCEPTING DIFFERENCES

The fear of labeling stems from a fear of prejudice. Not only is it important for teachers to know and care about children, it is important for them to accept differences. I realize this may sound trite and obvious, but what may not be obvious is that our educational system is not set up to accept and value differences. Can children disclose information about their disadvantaged backgrounds? Do teachers really value emotional intelligence? Do academics readily adopt and integrate new ideas (such as qualitative inquiry)? There are many ways that we subtly try to mold people to fit a traditional image and in this way we discourage difference.

To help students reach their full potential, teachers must strive to understand and value different types of intelligence. Most of the women in this project developed emotional intelligence at a young age. Even if a child has difficulty reading or calculating equations, this doesn't mean she can't think, she can't lead, she can't sing, she can't play soccer. Teachers often focus on only a few aspects of a child's intelligence and then transmits to him or her a sense of worth using only these criteria. Educators need to recognize and understand children's strengths and value them. They can concentrate on developing other skill areas after children have integrated the message that they are capable.

So far, I have talked about the difficulties in knowing students. I have also discussed the need for teachers to value intellectual differences. At this point, all we need to do is provide teachers with the time for developing relationships with their students and reflecting on those relationships and we also need to open teachers' minds so they no longer value only characteristics they were taught to value, but also those that are different. No problem, right?

ELIMINATING HIERARCHY

The idea of eliminating hierarchy (which is my next suggestion) seems more idealistic than knowing students and valuing intellectual differences. Many people like hierarchy. It provides a clear role for everyone, from top to bottom. With a hierarchy, everyone understands where she or he belongs. There is no confusion about who should make decisions and how those decisions should be carried out. Order replaces chaos. Also, as was mentioned earlier, many who are on the bottom accept their lower level positions with the hope that one day they will replace those in the top positions.

Women are the first to criticize hierarchical structures, which makes sense, since the traditional hierarchy has not always been fair to women. However, it is young women in academia who are the first to complain that college students expect more from them than they do from male professors (Basow & Silberg,1987; Caplan, 1994). Also, although most women academics believe that professors should have to earn the respect of their students, they get angry when students do not automatically respect them for their educational achievement and their experience. Women argue that students should feel comfortable enough to question a professor, but they become insecure and frustrated when students continually question their knowledge and abilities while continuing to be intimidated (and motivated) by those academics (mainly men) who function under a traditional hierarchy. Hierarchy does serve a real function in our society, and those who oppose this structure face wrath from those who benefit from it and more demands (and less respect) from people they hope to help by eliminating it.

MAKING CHANGES

So far in this chapter, my gloomy words have illustrated the complexities that are usually ignored as idealistic authors make sweeping announcements that teachers should know their students, value what students have to offer, and challenge the patriarchal hierarchy. However, I did promise to brighten this chapter with a positive example of a program that is actually achieving some of these goals. The Institute for Educational Transformation (IET) at George Mason University is an interdisciplinary, school-based master's program for teachers (Sockett, 1993). I have chosen to describe the IET program because it provides an excellent example of how educators can work together to make many of the changes that were outlined in this book.

The IET program was created to forge a better relationship between university faculty and K-12 teachers (Sockett, 1993). It is an alternative to the deficiencies of traditional programs, specifically the failure to bridge the gap between theory and practice, to improve student learning, and to facilitate collegial school cultures. To ensure that intellectual efforts are aimed at practice, teachers earn half their credits for research done in their own classrooms. To foster collaboration and avoid isolation, teachers enter the program in teams from individual schools. These teams start and finish the programs together over a period of two years and three months. To encourage the development of a learning community, the university faculty also teach in teams and follow the students throughout their stay in the program. To respect the scheduling demands of classroom teachers, IET holds two-week summer sessions and four full-day Saturday sessions during each school year. To further support teachers, IET has negotiated with school districts for teachers to receive four release days to attend classes during each school year. To enhance workplace-based study, faculty members visit school sites a few times each semester. To facilitate communication, laptop computers are provided for E-mail, electronic conferencing and other Internet use.

In content, the program confronts moral and epistemological issues that affect teachers' interpretations and judgments regarding their classrooms. To support critical reflection, teachers write autobiographies, narratives, and reflections on experience and then use multiple theoretical frameworks for interpreting them. To promote critical reading, teachers are given precourse requirements for reading imaginative literature; and thereafter engage with theory from several different disciplines. To enhance collegial dialog, teachers work collectively within and across teams to articulate the issues most salient to present practices. To foster ongoing inquiry into and documentation of practice, teachers undertake individual and group research projects centered on their workplaces.

The program itself provides an excellent example of a good professional development program for teachers, but what I'd like to emphasize is the struggles the college faculty go through daily to reinvent "a good educational program." They listen to feedback from students; they reflect on their personal biases, and they work hard to know students, care about students, understand differences and eliminate the traditional hierarchy. I was very annoyed when I first started working at IET because my colleagues kept reminding me that we call our students "the teachers." We do not call them "students." I thought this was ridiculous and a little overboard until one of the students told me that after being in our program for a while, she had never thought of herself as a student, but as a member of our learning community. I was surprised how proud I was of this particular compliment.

Many IET strategies clearly connect to the needs outlined by the women in this book. For example, the IET faculty struggle to allow the teachers to reveal who they are and connect their learning to personal experience by having them write autobiographies and narratives and then reflect on their experiences. The faculty strive to know students by meeting with them at their schools and talking with them electronically through E-mail and conferencing. They work to eliminate hierarchy and arrogance in higher education by creating equality among faculty team members including tenured faculty, contract faculty, part-time faculty, community members, staff, graduate assistants and K-12 faculty. They strive to make students feel confident in their abilities as they focus on higher level thinking and moral decision making. They are open to new ideas, such as strategies in teaming, new techniques in research and technology, and new ideas in curriculum. They reach out to the community through their site-based master's and other community-based programs to appropriately involve community members, parents, administrators and children. And most important, they continue to work to improve the program even after facing setbacks, which are unavoidable when working to transform education. The faculty's goal is to model for the teachers the type of educational program they should be developing in their own classrooms. The IET faculty is constantly struggling to reinvent professional development by reflecting on what works and what doesn't. They do not always reach their goals, and often their communication breaks down, but I have been impressed with the way they continue to struggle to provide an appropriate and effective educational experience for their students.

SUMMARY AND CONCLUSION

As I reflect on how we should transform education, it is fairly easy to summarize the changes the women in this book wanted from schools, but it is not so easy to bring about these changes. Still, knowing what high achievers liked and didn't like about their educational experience can provide insights into what works in schools and what doesn't. Since these women have always been on the bottom of an abusive hierarchy, they have difficulty with this particular structure. These women want teachers and mentors who treat them as future colleagues and who value what they bring to their educational experience. They want educators to care about them and know them as people. They want to be challenged in their thinking and validated for their intellectual style. These women prefer a type of learning that is independent. When professors allow students to be independent, it is a sign that they trust them to know what they need to learn and where to start. They want educators to encourage them to start their learning process from personal experience and move in other directions from there. They want traditional methods and basic skills to be acknowledged as being "traditional" and "basic." They want to be evaluated accurately, according to their own strengths. As children, they want to be recognized as special and smart. They want the schools to get to know their parents and family situations in a way that does not embarrass or stigmatize them. And finally, they want more connection with the broader community.

In a social psychology textbook, the author states that group differences are often exaggerated (Meyers, 1993). This is probably true. Although the intention of this book was to explore the experiences of women who were disadvantaged, many of the conclusions in this book apply to other students. For example, the women who were interviewed were offended by arrogance in higher education. Earlier, it was suggested that traditional students may be more comfortable with the culture in higher education. Still, this does not mean that traditional students would prefer arrogance and elitism. Although Belenky and her colleagues (1986) did not interview only high-achieving women from disadvantaged backgrounds, in their attempt to understand the needs of women generally in higher education, their participants described needs similar to those outlined here. In another example, Poplin and Stone (1992), two researchers who have studied the needs of special learners, have described a paradigm that they called "Holistic Constructivism." In this paradigm, educators, feminists and critical pedagogists tend to de-emphasize development limitations and emphasize the role of primary language affect, intuition, and sociopolitical forces in learning.

They stress the role of interest, self-concept, connectedness, trust, and expectations in learning. It is important to point out that what these researchers consider important in the process of transforming education are the same as those I've been emphasizing in this book, even though we study the needs of different groups of people.

The problems today in providing protective interventions for disadvantaged children do not arise because we lack consensus that something needs to be done. The problems are that we do not know how to define disadvantage, we do not recognize and acknowledge the diversity in children's disadvantages, we do not have the resources to provide necessary services. Further, when services are provided, they are defined narrowly, without respect for individual needs, and they are stated idealistically, with no regard for the realities associated with making significant changes.

At one time during my doctoral program in education, I was at a college party and after explaining to a fellow graduate student what I was doing with my life, she asked me what I planned to do about our failing educational system. Her question threw me off guard. This was not an easy question to answer quickly in front of a group of a party-goers. I have thought about this question since that embarrassing moment and if I could answer her today, I would say that it comes down to values. Everyone is responsible for education, not just doctoral students, K-12 teachers, university professors or parents. Everyone is responsible and should be involved in bettering education. Schools should be better funded, teachers should be better compensated, parents and community members should be more involved.

The women I interviewed for this project were motivated by the same goal. They wanted to help make the achievement process less difficult for those who walk beside them and those who will follow in their footsteps. They gave time and energy with no expectations of immediate reward. Ultimately, education will be transformed when a large percentage of the population shows an interest in bettering our educational system with the same selfless dedication exhibited by the women in this book!

Appendix A

DEMOGRAPHICS

Stress List

As a child, have you ever yourself directly, or indirectly (with family or significant others) experienced these stressful life events? (check all that apply)

_____alcoholism

_____drug abuse

_____physical abuse

_____sexual abuse

_____emotional abuse

_____mental illness

_____constant parental strife

_____divorce

_____homelessness

_____death of a parent

_____death of both parents

_____death of a sibling

_____death of a significant other

_____rape

_____other violent crimes

_____incarceration

_____war or violent political strife within your country

_____migrant lifestyle or constant moving

_____one-parent household

_____discrimination

_____poverty

_____serious illness

_____disability

Table A.1
Demographic Information and Risk Profile

Par.	Age	Ethnicity	SES	Level of educ. for mother	Level of educ. for father	List of stressors checked
A	37	African-American	lower	high school	5th grade	alcoholism, drug abuse, poverty, physical abuse, emotional abuse, mental illness, parental strife, rape, other violent crimes, incarceration, political strife, discrimination
B	29	Chicana	working or lower	high school/ some college at age 50	high school	alcoholism, emotional & physical abuse, discrimination, incarceration, poverty
C	37	European-American	lower middle or working	high school/ some college	high school/ some college	alcoholism, drug abuse, rape, physical abuse, sexual abuse, emotional abuse, parental strife, homelessness, other violent crimes, war/political strife, serious illness, migrant life/moving, disability, death of an extended family in house
D	26	European-American	working	high school	GED	alcoholism, parental strife

128

	Age	Ethnicity	SES	Education	Education	Stressors
E	37	European-American	middle	high school/ attended college for 3 yrs.	high school/ graduate from trade school	alcoholism, drug abuse, physical & emotional abuse, mental illness, parental strife, divorce, violent crime, one-parent household, serious illness
F	28	European-American	Ranged from lower to upper	high school/ 2 yrs. technical	did not graduate from high school	alcoholism, drug abuse, poverty, physical abuse, emotional, disability, serious illness, parental strife, incarceration, one-parent household, serious illness
G	44	European-American	lower middle or working	2 yrs of college after children were grown	high school	alcoholism, parental strife
H	54	European-American	lower/ welfare family	4th grade educ.	8th grade educ.	alcoholism, emotional abuse, death of a parent, death of a sibling, poverty, serious illness, infant deaths
I	46	European-American	working or lower	high school	7th grade	alcoholism, drug abuse (sib), physical abuse (sib), emotional strife/parent and sib, poverty, incarceration (sib), disability, constant moving, neglect

Table A.1 (continued)

J	38	European-American	lower	high school/ later nursing degree	high school	sexual abuse , poverty
K	36	European-American/ immigrant from Germany	middle	high school	high school	drug abuse, physical abuse, emotional abuse, disability
L	31	European-American	middle	high school	high school	alcoholism, physical abuse, emotional abuse, serious illness, death of both parents (15, 20), death of sibling, serious illness
M	24	European-American	lower working	did not grad from high	did not grad from high	alcoholism, parental strife, drug abuse, gambling, physical abuse, sexual abuse, emotional abuse
N	26	Hispanic	lower middle or working	high school/ 1 yr. of college	6th grade	alcoholism, physical abuse, emotional abuse, parental strife, divorce, one-parent household, poverty
O	30	European-American	lower middle or working	high school	high school	sexual abuse, emotional abuse, parental strife, serious illness, disability

	Age	Ethnicity	Class	Education	Education	Difficult Experiences
P	34	African-American	lower middle or working	high school	high school	alcoholism, drug use, divorce, discrimination, serious illness, attempted suicide
Q	39	European-American	middle	high school	high school and 1 year after high	alcoholism, physical abuse, sexual abuse, emotional abuse, parental strife, divorce, death of a significant other, one-parent household, disability, attempted suicide
R	47	European-American	lower middle or working (moved up later)	high school	GED and some college later in his life	alcoholism, drug abuse, disability, suicide, physical abuse, emotional abuse, mental illness (mother), divorce, parental strife, death of a parent, death of a significant other, rape, other violent crimes, incarceration (sib), political strife, one parent household, illness
S	38	European-American	lower middle or working	high school	did not grad from high	alcoholism, parental strife, death of a parent, serious illness
T	26	European-American	from lower middle working	associate degree in liberal arts	high school and voc.school	death of a parent, serious illness, one-parent household
U	32	European-American	middle	high school	did not grad from high	drug abuse, physical abuse, sexual abuse, emotional abuse, parental strife, divorce, migrant/moving, discrimination, poverty, serious illness

Table A.2
Education Profile

No.	Undergraduate (BA, BS)	Masters (MS, MA, MBA)	Doctorate
PA	Speech Pathology	Speech Pathology	Speech Pathology
PB	Business	Business	Social and Cultural Studies in Education
PC	Broadcast Journalism	Clinical Psychology	
PD	Communication	Communication	
PE	Psychology	Business/Marketing	
PF	Psychology	International Education	Special Education
PG	Philosophy and Russian	Divinity	Comparative Near Eastern Religions
PH	Psychology	Psychology	Psychology
PI	History	Counseling Psychology	Psychology
PJ	English	Business/Marketing	
PK	Organizational Behavior/ Business	English as Second Language and Financial Planning	
PL	Biology	Biology	Biology
PM	Psychology	School Psychology	
PN	Business	Public Administration	
PO	Art	Architecture	
PP	Physiology and Health Arts and Sciences	Community Public Health	Community Public Health
PQ	Journalism	Educational Administration	Education
PR	English	Research Psychology	Special Education
PS	Political Science	International Relations	
PT	Psychology	Epidemiology	Social Psychology
PU	English Literature	English Composition	

Table A.3
Geographic Profile

Colleges and Universities Attended (Where participants attended school as undergraduate students or graduate students)	States/Countries (Where participants grew up as children)	Cities (Where participants grew up as children)
University of California, Berkeley	California	Highland, IN
University of California, Riverside	Minnesota	Pleasanton, CA
Franciscan School of Theology	Ohio	West Islip, NY
Graduate Theological Union	Indiana	Oshkosh, WI
University of Minnesota	Massachusetts	San Francisco, CA
John F. Kennedy University	New Hampshire	El Sobranto, CA
University of Wisconsin, Oshkosh	Utah	La Gloria Tiajuana, Mex.
The College of Wooster	Arkansas	San Diego, CA
San Francisco State University	Idaho	Worchester, MA
Dartmouth College	Maryland	Formosa, Japan
South Lake Tahoe Community College	Kentucky	Oakland, CA
San Diego State University	Virginia	Los Angeles, CA
University of Virginia	Illinois	Boise, ID
Harvard University	New York	Washington, DC
University of Maine, at Farmington	Wisconsin	Chino, CA
University of Central Florida	Iowa	Alberthea, MN
Colorado State University		Minneapolis, MN
Wright State University	Japan	Modesto, CA
Indiana University	Mexico	Turlock, CA
Yale University	Germany	Charles City, IA
Southern Illinois University		Roosevelt, UT
State University of New York, at Brockport		Citrus Heights, CA

Table A.3 (continued)

Chabot College		Boston, MA
University of the District of Columbia		Bridgewater, NH
Boise State University		Walnut Creek, AR
University of California, Los Angeles		Coldwater, OH
California State University, Fullerton		
University of California, Irvine		
University of Southern California		
St. Mary's College		
California State University, Hayward		
University of San Diego		
San Diego Mesa College		
California Polytechnic, Pomona		
College of the Desert		
Hebrew University of Jerusalem		
University of Nebraska		
Syracuse University		
California State University, Stanislaus		

Note: Some of the participants did not list the cities where they grew up, only the states. This was due to constant moving within that state.

134

Appendix B

DATA COLLECTION METHODS

IN-DEPTH INTERVIEWS

Data were collected in three ways: through in-depth interviews, questionnaires and historical records. In-depth personal interviews were used to describe and explain the educational experiences of each participant. These interviews provided the opportunity to explore in detail each participant's ideas and feelings about her education. The interviews were open-ended; the interviewer guided the inquiry, but the participants were allowed to discuss in detail what they considered important about their lives and their educational experiences. The interview protocol was organized in a way that allowed participants to broadly describe their experiences. For example, one of the first requests was "Tell me about your experience in elementary school." As the participants brought up certain issues, the interviewer probed deeply into the topic. Inevitably, the women spent more time talking about "their experience in elementary school" than they had originally thought possible. This procedure gave the participants the opportunity to remember issues that were most relevant for them first, and then the interviewer followed their lead. After the participants finished discussing their experiences chronologically, they were asked more specific questions, such as "how do you feel about standardized tests?" or "were you ever involved in programs for disadvantaged children?" The interviews were audiotaped and then transcribed verbatim in preparation for analysis.

The participants had the opportunity to choose the location of the interview. They had the choice of meeting at their home, their office, the interviewer's home, an office provided by the school, or any other location, as long as it was quiet and private. The interviews were conducted in many different locations depending on what was convenient for each participant.

QUESTIONNAIRE

After the interview was completed, an experience questionnaire was administered to each participant. The design of this questionnaire was guided by pilot study findings. In fact, six categories emerged from the pilot study, and questions related to each category were included in the questionnaire (see experience questionnaire in Appendix C). The questionnaire provided a second opportunity in a completely different format, for the participants to express their attitudes about their education. Occasionally the questions from the questionnaire reminded participants of an educational experience. In these situations, women were allowed to continue their verbal discussion, and the audio tape was turned back on.

TRANSCRIPTS

Historical records were also used to illuminate the participant's stories. Participants were asked to sign a letter of permission so that the investigator could send away for transcripts from high schools, colleges and graduate schools. By analyzing transcripts, not only was I able to study actual records along with self-report data, but these records were also used to identify the types of classes taken by individual students, grade levels in certain subjects, patterns of class enrollment, and elements of transition from high school to college.

At the end of the pilot study interview, some of the women were concerned that they may have left out important information. So a follow-up questionnaire, with an addressed envelope, was given to each participant to take home in case they wished to report additional information after the interview. If the women had more to say, they could send back the information sheet with additional comments. Also, if the women found they had more to say after the interview, they were encouraged to continue the conversation, either on the telephone or in person. One woman asked to meet a second time to continue discussing issues. Several women (six) sent back the follow-up questionnaires, which provided additional thoughts and experiences.

DATA ANALYSIS

The challenge of qualitative data analysis is to make sense of massive amounts of data, identify significant patterns, and construct a framework for communicating the essence of what the data reveal (Patton, 1990). First, transcripts were made from each interview, and descriptive data was presented in such a way that people could draw their own conclusions. For example, dialog quotes were coded and listed as evidence, and demographic information was presented in tables.

Interviews were analyzed with an inductive cross-case analysis. Inductive analysis means that the patterns, themes and categories emerged out of the data rather than being imposed on them prior to data collection and analysis. A cross-case analysis means that the information was grouped together according to answers from different people, themes, perspectives or issues. Then, a content analysis was conducted; this included the process of identifying, coding, and categorizing the primary patterns in the data. After that process, a case record was developed. The participants' case records included all the most important information used in the final analysis. Information was edited, redundancies were sorted out, parts were fitted together, and the case record was organized for ready access. In this project, data were organized topically.

In the final step, the data were interpreted. Interpretation, by definition, goes beyond description. Interpretation means attaching significance to what was found, offering explanations, drawing conclusions, making inferences, building linkages, attaching meanings, imposing order and dealing with rival explanations. For example, when interpreting interview data, the goal is to capture pieces of dialog, organize these quotes, develop a theme and then deduce a meaning from that theme. Sometimes an investigator can do this from what is said directly, and sometimes from what is said indirectly. For example, here is a statement made by one of the participants:

Being understood as an emotional person—particularly as a kid, I've never thought about this before, so I can't think through what that might have been like —to have somebody who was there, not to heal me, but just to understand *who I was* and then make me learn *despite it.*

This statement would indicate there was something wrong with who this woman was as a child. What she probably meant to say was that she wanted someone to understand what she was going through and help her learn despite her difficulties. This could be an isolated incident or, if other similar comments were found, it could suggest a pattern. In this case, an investigator may look for a pattern of low self-esteem.

At this point, it is important for me to take responsibility for my interpretations and make a clear distinction between description and interpretation. It is also important to state the strengths and weaknesses of this method of inquiry. In qualitative research the emphasis is on illumination, understanding and extrapolation rather than causal determination, prediction and generalization.

RIGOR

Within the positivist paradigm, a study's rigor is judged through measures of reliability and validity. Lincoln and Guba (1985) however, present a strong case against the use of these terms within a qualitative paradigm since the purpose of qualitative research is to further understanding without reference to causality. In response, Lincoln and Guba have offered the following four alternative terms, which are more applicable in determining the rigor of a study conducted within an interpretivistic paradigm: credibility, comfirmability, dependability and transferability.

Credibility refers to the researcher's ability to conduct the study in a manner that ensures that the participant is accurately identified and described. In other words, credibility refers to the believability or the confidence of the study. Researchers historically have not trusted self-report data. Listed below are examples of problems associated with this form of information gathering:

*   People often remember only the traumatic.
*   People color the truth to make themselves look better.
*   People forget important information.
*   People have trouble remembering information accurately.
*   People give different testimony depending upon the interviewer, the time of the interview and the environment.

The interview data were illuminated with information provided in the questionnaires and in other historical documentation (transcripts). It should be emphasized, however, that the most important information gathered from this study relates to memories that are apparent. It is the goal of this study to understand the most dramatic experiences in these women's education and determine how those experiences influenced their achievement.

As an additional check on credibility, the women in this study were given a copy of the final report and asked to provide feedback on whether or not the results accurately reflected their voices. The women's comments are listed in Appendix D.

In qualitative research, investigators also strive for *confirmability*. It is important to determine whether the findings can be confirmed by another researcher. To check my interpretations of the women's interviews, two outside observers (in addition to the research committee members) were asked to evaluate the interpretations. Both outside observers were men. One is a psychologist who has 5 years of clinical experience; the second has a Ph.D. in mechanical engineering. It was determined that by allowing the interpretations to be checked by two people with perspectives other than that of the researcher, additional objectivity was added to the evaluation process. These two observers were asked to examine the dialog quotes and other evidence to determine whether consistent analysis and objective interpretations were presented.

Dependability refers to the researcher's attempts to account for changing conditions in the phenomenon chosen for study as well as changes in the design created by an increasingly refined understanding of the setting. This represents a set of assumptions very different from those shaping the concept of reliability. Positivists' notions of reliability assume an unchanging universe where an inquiry could be replicated. Interpretivists believe that the social world is always changing and the concept of replication is itself problematic (Marshall & Rossman, 1989) It was seldom necessary to make changes during the investigation. However, the interviews were open-ended, and although the focus of this research was on educational influences, the women often talked about influences from their home and from the community. I decided during the study that these women should be allowed to discuss relevant issues whether or not they related to education. As a result, a chapter on family and community influences was added to the book. To account for dependability, overlapping methods were used. Interviews, questionnaires and historical information served to corroborate and clarify data.

Finally, *transferability* refers to the applicability of the findings to other settings, contexts and groups. The results of this study cannot be generalized to other women who have achieved highly in academics and were also disadvantaged as children. Neither was this the purpose of the study. However, by using detailed information that was gathered through multiple methods, other researchers can explore the data and the results and determine the applicability of the findings to their specific situations. Triangulation of methods through the use of multiple cases, multiple outside observers, multiple sources of data and multiple theories strengthen's the transferability of the results of this study (Lincoln, 1988).

Appendix C

RESEARCH TABLES

EXPERIENCE QUESTIONNAIRE

To augment the participants' interview data, a questionnaire allowed the women to describe their educational experiences in a different format. The benefits of the questionnaire were two-fold. First, it provided a consistency check. Second, the questionnaire provided more evidence to support or dispute interpretations made from the interview data. The questionnaire was developed from results obtained from a pilot study. Therefore, the questions posed relate to many of the conclusions derived from the pilot study's interview data. The questionnaire was given to the participants after the initial interview so that it would not bias their testimonies.

The experience questionnaire supported much of the data presented in the interviews, although many participants tended to be more reserved when answering questions on the questionnaire than they were when answering similar questions in the interview. There are several possible reasons why this might have happened. For one, often the women chose an answer that represented a compromise rather than a clear indication of their feelings. For example, some of the women liked competition when they were young, but did not like it as adults. Others liked competing against themselves, but did not like competing with other students. When choosing whether or not they "liked" or "disliked" competition in the questionnaire, they were unsure how to present their complex feelings given only three possible answers: yes, somewhat and no. Luckily, they had the option to discuss the questionnaire as they selected answers. However, after they explained their answers, they still had to select one of the three choices provided. In this, and other similar situations, the women often compromised and selected the choice that indicated they "somewhat" liked competition. Also, a few times, the women chose not to provide answers for certain questions. Since this was a qualitative study, where the questionnaire was being used mainly as a consistency check, if the women did not feel they could accurately represent their voices by answering a specific question, they were not forced to answer the question.

It should also be mentioned that some of the interpretations of the interview data were based on statements that revealed unconscious patterns. Therefore, conclusions from the interview data were often made from extrapolation, not always from direct quotes. A questionnaire usually cannot reveal this type of pattern because participants most often answer questions according to conscious attitudes.

Ultimately, none of the questionnaire data disputed the interpretations presented from the interview data. In fact, some examples of how the questionnaire data clearly supported the interview data are listed below:

- Participants believed disadvantage had negative connotations
- There was no clear consensus on what was important in teaching style
- Participants did well in school and were recognized for their achievements
- A majority of participants did not have counseling and mentoring at any level, especially emotional mentors
- Participants were not comfortable talking about their disadvantage
- Participants were ambivalent about their families, on question #34, fourteen of the participants claimed that someone in their family was especially influential in a positive way, and then in question #35, 14 participants claimed that they achieved despite their family.
- In question 37, participants show that a majority had a sense of belonging in elementary school and in graduate school and did not in high school and college. This supports the achievement pattern outlined in Chapter 9.
- A majority of women claimed they did not believe standardized tests accurately measured their abilities, although a larger number of participants claimed they did fairly well or somewhat well on standardized tests as represented in question 12.

Table C.1
Scores from the Experience Questionnaire

	Yes	Somewhat	No
Defining disadvantage			
1) Do you believe that you were disadvantaged as a child?	13	6	2
2) Do you believe that the word disadvantage has bad connotations?	17	1	3
3) Do you believe that your disadvantage has negatively affected your academic achievement?	2	8	10
4) Do you believe that your disadvantage has positively affected your academic achievement?	7	10	3
Teaching			
5) Did the teaching style of different instructors significantly affect your achievement in?			
high school	12	6	3
college (as an undergraduate)	11	6	4
graduate school	9	8	4
6) Did you like academic competition?			
in high school	6	8	7
in college (as an undergraduate)	5	9	7
in graduate school	7	6	8
7) Did you like cooperative learning groups?			
in high school	7	5	4
in college (as an undergraduate)	8	6	5
in graduate school	12	7	1
8) Did you like lecture-based presentation?			
in high school	11	3	7
in college (as an undergraduate)	10	6	5
in graduate school	7	7	7

Table C.1 (continued)

Expectations

9) Were you ever recognized for outstanding achievement in?

high school	16	2	3
college (as an undergraduate)	12	3	6
graduate school	8	6	7

10) Did you earn good grades in? (your definition)

high school	12	6	3
college (as an undergraduate)	12	5	4
graduate school	15	4	1

11) Did other people always expect you to do well in?

high school	15	1	5
college (as an undergraduate)	13	0	8
graduate school	14	2	5

12) Did you do well on standardized achievement tests?

for admission to college (as an undergraduate)	12	6	3
for admission to graduate school	8	5	7

Support

13) Did you get academic counseling in high school?	4	5	12

14) Did a professional at your school serve as an academic mentor in?

high school	4	4	13
college (as an undergraduate)	7	3	11
graduate school	10	1	10

15) Did a professional at your school serve as an emotional mentor in?

high school	2	2	17
college (as an undergraduate)	1	5	15
graduate school	5	3	13

16) Did you feel supported by teachers in?

high school	9	6	6
college (as an undergraduate)	8	5	8
graduate school	11	4	6

17) Did you make the right decision about the schools in?

college (as an undergraduate)	11	5	5
graduate school	19	2	0

18) Did you make the right choice of majors in?

college (as an undergraduate)	14	2	5
graduate school	18	1	2

19) Did you have any financial assistance in?

high school	5	1	14
college (as an undergraduate)	14	6	1
graduate school	14	1	6

20) Did you feel that you had enough financial assistance in?

high school	12	2	5
college (as an undergraduate)	12	3	6
graduate school	8	3	10

Issues of Class Race and Gender

21) Did you feel that you encountered any issues related to your race that had a **negative** effect on your experience in?

high school	3	1	17
college (as an undergraduate)	2	4	15
graduate school	1	3	17

Table C.1 (continued)

22) Did you feel that you encountered any issues related to your gender that had a **negative** effect on your experience in?			
high school	10	2	9
college (as an undergraduate)	5	3	13
graduate school	5	7	9
23) Did you feel that you encountered any issues related to your disadvantage that had a **negative** effect on your experience in?			
high school	9	6	5
college (as an undergraduate)	5	6	9
graduate school	6	3	11
24) Did you feel that you encountered any issues related to your race that had a **positive** effect on your experience in?			
high school	4	3	14
college (as an undergraduate)	6	4	11
graduate school	6	4	11
25) Did you feel that you encountered any issues related to your gender that had a **positive** effect on your experience in?			
high school	4	5	11
college (as an undergraduate)	4	5	11
graduate school	6	5	9
26) Did you encounter issues related to your disadvantage that positively affected your experience in?			
high school	2	3	15
college (as an undergraduate)	4	3	13
graduate school	5	2	12

27) Were you comfortable talking about personal experience related to your disadvantage in?

high school	3	2	16
college (as an undergraduate)	2	6	12
graduate school	8	3	9

28) Were you ever asked about your disadvantage in?

high school	2	1	17
college (as an undergraduate)	1	0	19
graduate school	3	3	14

29) Did you believe that any school official knew you as an individual in?

high school	10	4	7
college (as an undergraduate)	9	6	6
graduate school	11	4	6

Family

30) Did your family provide information about education?	3	4	14
31) Was your family supportive of your education?	7	10	4
32) Were your parents as supportive of women in the family as they were of the men?	9	2	7
33) Did your family provide any financial resources?	5	11	5
34) Was one or more persons in your family especially influential?	14	0	7
35) Do you believe that you achieved in spite of your family?	14	4	3

Overall Experience of School

36) Did you enjoy?

elementary school	15	6	0
high school	9	6	6
college (as an undergraduate)	13	5	3
graduate school	16	4	1

147

Table C.1 (continued)

37) Did you feel a sense of belonging in:			
elementary school	11	8	2
high school	4	9	8
college (as an undergraduate)	6	9	6
graduate school	15	4	2
38) Did you get nervous when you were interviewed by a school representative in?			
high school	7	1	8
college (as an undergraduate)	7	6	4
graduate school	5	6	6
39) Did you get nervous when you spoke aloud in class in?			
high school	7	6	8
college (as an undergraduate)	6	9	6
graduate school	5	10	6
40) Did you feel comfortable stating opinions in class in?			
high school	12	5	4
college (as an undergraduate)	10	7	4
graduate school	11	7	3
41) Do you believe a standardized achievement test is a good method to evaluate students' abilities?	3	6	11
42) Do you believe that you have been evaluated accurately in?			
high school	9	6	6
college (as an undergraduate)	11	8	2
graduate school	13	6	2

148

Table C.2
Number and Type of Transcripts Received

Name Code	High School	College	Grad.
1A	X	X	X
2B		X	X
3C	X	X	X
4D		X	XX
5D	X	XXXX	X
6D		XX	
7E		XX	
8F	X	X	X
9G	X	X	X
10H		X	XX
11I		XX	XX
12K		X	XX
13L	X	X	XX
14M	X	X	X
15N	X	X	
16O	X	X	XX
17P	X		X
18Q	X	XX	
19R		X	
20S		X	

Table C.3
Voice Representation Table: Number of Quotes from Each Participant Presented as Evidence in Each Chapter in the Original Report.

#	Chap. 4 Relation with disadv.	Chap. 3 Personality	Chap. 5 Teachers	Chap. 6 Mentors	Chap. 8 Negative aspects of schooling	Chap. 7 Positive aspects of schooling	Chap. 9 Achieve develop patterns	Chap. 10 Family and comm.	Total	# pages on transc.	# of Quotes per page
1	III	IIII	II	IIII	IIIIII	II	IIII	IIIII	31	133	.23
2	IIII	III	II	III	III	II		III	20	78	.26
3	IIIII	IIII	II	II	IIII	I	II	IIII	24	63	.38
4	I		IIIIII	I	I		I	II	12	57	.21
5			IIII	I	II	I	I	II	11	60	.18
6	IIII	I	IIII	III	III	IIIII	I	IIII	25	103	.24
7	II	I	I	I	II	I	IIII	IIIII	17	75	.23
8	I	II	II	I	I	I	II	III	13	55	.24
9	IIIIII	IIIII	III	I	IIII	IIIII	IIIII	III	33	56	.59
10	I	III	I		III	II	II	IIIII	18	124	.14
11	IIIIII	IIIIIII	I	IIII	III	II	IIII	IIII	35	122	.29
12	II	IIII	IIIII	I	IIIIII	I	III	IIII	28	112	.23
13	III	I	IIIII	II			I		12	41	.29
14	II	II	III	I	IIII	IIII	I	IIII	21	79	.27
15	III			I	III	I	III	IIIIII	18	81	.22
16	IIII	II	III	IIII	III	II		IIII	23	77	.30
17	IIII	IIII	III	III	IIIIIII		IIIIIII	IIII	39	148	.26
18	II	II	II	II	III	III	II	III	22	83	.27
19	I	IIII		IIII		IIII	I	II	18	71	.25
20	IIII		IIIII	II	III		I	II	18	80	.23
21	IIII	III	III	II	IIII	II		IIIII	23	119	.19

Table C.4
Two Examples of Consistency Tables: Comparing Interviews, Questionnaires and Transcripts

Statements (Participant # 1)	Interview	Exper.	Demog.	Trans.
Earned good grades graduate school/slightly above in college/major changed in college	T1P99L10	10		Gr, Co
Bad high school counseling	T1P30L16	13		
Specific grade in calculus (graduate school)	T1P70L3			Gr
Sibling's problems (incarceration, drug, alcohol)	T1P81L19	35	Stress list	
Sense of belonging in graduate school (improved)	T1P105L16	37		

Statements (Participant # 2)	Interview	Exper.	Demo.	Transc.
Exact number of students in graduating class (63)	T2P14L21			HS
Grades 1st semester college (all B's) mentioned two classes: chemistry and philosophy	T2P36L9			Co
Won scholarships as an undergraduate	T2P35L11	19		
Poverty/welfare was the disadvantage	T2P4L8	1	stress list	
Liked lecture as an undergraduate/less so in grad.	T2P73L3	8		

Exper.--Experience Questionnaire
Demo.--Demographic Questionnaire
Transc.--Transcripts

HS.--High school Transcripts
Gr.--Graduate School Transcripts
Co.--Undergraduate Transcripts

Appendix D

FEEDBACK QUESTIONNAIRE AND PARTICIPANTS' COMMENTS

FEEDBACK QUESTIONNAIRE

Please select one of the choices listed below:

<u>9</u>   Most of my experiences were very well represented in this research study.
<u>2</u>   Many of my experiences were well represented in this study.
____Some of my experiences were well represented and some were not.
____Some of my experiences were represented well, but most were not.
____Most of my experiences were not represented well in this study.
____Other, list comments below.

Please select one of the choices listed below:

<u>6</u>   I agree with almost all of the interpretations made in this research study.
<u>5</u>   I agree with most of the interpretations made in this research study.
____I agree with many of the interpretations made in this research study.
____I agree with some of the interpretations made in this research study.
____I only agreed with a few of the interpretations made in this research study.
____I disagreed with most of the interpretations made in this research study.
____Other, list comments below.

Eleven women responded. When the report was sent to each woman, I indicated that they had the choice to provide feedback or not. However, if they did not provide feedback, I would assume their voice was represented well.

COMMENTS ABOUT HOW WELL THEIR VOICES WERE REPRESENTED:

Maria: I think that my voice was well represented in this study.

Toni: I really enjoyed reading this study. It was interesting and amusing to see myself quoted alongside, within and among others. Many of your interpretations hit the nail on the head. For example, attitudes which motivate children and families to hide dysfunction rang true for me.

Janet: In sum, it was validating to read of other women's experiences and to realize there's a whole closet community of us out there. I hope your study can be of help to others out there.

Helen: Thank you for sending the results of your study. I appreciate hearing what others said and how you interpreted our material. In reading the quotes of the other participants, I found that many things that others said, I could have said too. I think you have done an excellent job of interpreting our material, and I can't say how glad I am to see such a study be done.

Toni: Thank you for the study. It was very validating to participate. I hope your results can be useful.

No Identification: I was very impressed with how similar my experiences and attitudes were to the other participants in the study, both in terms of the interpretations and the quoted passages.

Sara: I'm really impressed by the study; as I said when you interviewed me, this seems like a really important area of research, and you've done an excellent job.

Thoughts about their experience after reading the results and interpretations of this study:

Martha: I always felt incompetent—that's what's behind the drive to always do more, to succeed, and yet I never was satisfied. I've had to learn to appreciate my success.

Toni: I still have a strong desire to deny that I fall into this study group. First and foremost, I do not feel like I was disadvantaged. I feel like my childhood stresses were no big deal. In fact, I often deny that the abuse in my family, death of my parents, emotional physical and sexual abuse in my family ever happened. When I saw your risk profiles and I said to myself, "That's not me." Then, the next day when I saw my therapist, I showed it to her. We went over every single stress listed as mine, discussed it— yes, that is me.

Second, I don't feel like I've excelled. In fact, I have stopped writing my dissertation and may, or most likely, never complete it. So I really feel like I am not an example of success or resiliency and my achievement pattern doesn't fit since I haven't done "very well" in graduate school. I may add, though, that since I derive such security from being a student—to me success is being able to stay in school as long as possible—by that standard I have done "very well" in graduate school since I've managed to drag it out for nine years!

Janet: On gender issues, I have an alternate explanation for the younger women reporting less sexism. While I'd like to believe it's because things have now changed, it may just be that they haven't yet lived long enough to discern the pattern. I didn't recognize it until my mid to late 20s; it is easier to recognize after school. (In school, things are more objective.)

Tina: Very interesting stuff.

No identification: I did think there was a problem with the issue of whether the women are actually underprepared or only feel like they are underprepared, or both. Here, some references to actual achievement are needed to tell them apart. It is a very different thing to lack confidence in one's abilities, compared to knowing that you have entered a program without the usual prerequisites, as was my situation with respect to math. In the text, you seemed to waver between these two possibilities. I think different informants may have differed on this and you needed to use empirical info. to justify concluding an actual lack of preparation rather than sticking to your analysis of phenomenology, as you did in the rest of the discussion.

SPECIFIC FEEDBACK AS PRESENTED BY A PARTICIPANT IN A LETTER:

Dear Pam,

Thank you for sending the results of your study. I appreciate hearing what others said and how you interpreted our material. In reading the quotes of the other participants, I found that many things that others said, I could have said too. After reading your material, I find that I have much more to say. You are certainly welcome to use any of what I will say in this letter, if you wish. I think you have done an excellent job of interpreting our material, and I can't say how glad I am to see such a study be done. Now, about what I wanted to add . . .

(1) Let me begin by saying that I have been trying, over the past 40 years, to understand what happened in my childhood. In your terms, I have been trying to understand the nature of my disadvantage. You were right in quoting me as saying that for me poverty was the stress. However, when I rethink it, I realize that definition—that poverty was the reason for the all the bad things and the reason why I should not expect much from life—was said to me over and over when I was growing up. It probably was true that poverty was responsible for a lot of my difficulty. But, I m certain now, that it did not account for all of the problems and obstacles that I encountered. In recent years, I have begun to think that much more was wrong. In fact, reading the other participants' remarks, looking at my own in the context of theirs, and hearing your analysis and synthesis makes me understand better the extent and nature of the problems I faced in my youth.

My self-assessment over the past few years has led me to believe that my mother may have been mentally ill for much of her life. Her behavior (as I and my older sister remember it) is more understandable when viewed from that perspective. My father, although present in our home until his death when I was 17, actually was "absent" all along. His attitude seemed to be that we children belonged to our mother; we were her problem. While she was verbally and psychologically abusive, he mostly had nothing much to do with us. The best parenting I received came from my sister, who is 13 years older than I. The school also played a part of negligence in all of this. As far as I know, there was never any interference (or intervention) from the school in what was happening at home. Maybe they didn't know, but I think they didn't care. It is still the stance of this society that kids belong to their parents and that institutions like education have no right to intrude unless the maltreatment is severe and has physical signs.

(2) I was struck by your finding that high school was the worst time for most of us. For me, high school was bad because of a couple of things. First, at my puberty, my mother became especially abusive and the abuse continued until I graduated (at which time my father died). Second, during my teens, I became severely depressed; what I remember is that this was about having such a bleak future.

During high school, I, like some other of your participants, escaped from my mother by going to school, but in fact, my escape was never perfect. I never knew what kind of mood she'd be in when I came home; more often, she was in a bad mood and mad at me, and I would anticipate this while I was still at school. Like another participant, my mother also routinely berated me, called me names. According to her I was lazy, I was selfish, I was a slut, I was no good. I internalized her assessment of me.

My escape from her was also not perfect because she frequently prevented me from going to school. For example, I used to miss the first 4 to 6 weeks of school at the beginning of the term. . . in order to work in the fields (farm labor) to earn money for school clothes and supplies. (This was in support of the "poverty" explanation for why things weren't better; you can't go to school unless you have money...and you can't get money unless you stay out of school.) Further, during the school year it was not uncommon for her to keep me out so that I could help her do something (like laundry). She did this with my older siblings also; in fact, she found more reasons for them to stay out of school, so much so that it became more reasonable for them to just drop out. At one point, only a few months before I was to graduate, she wanted me to get married; I may have told you this. I knew that if I got married, this would mean that I would have to drop out of school, and I didn't want to. It was only because my father finally did intervene that she did not force me to.

Certainly, the school did not help (they did not know). I'm sure they would not have helped even if they had known; kids were allowed to drop out of school after 8th grade with absolutely no questions asked.

There was no encouragement of us to do well in school. It didn't really matter if you got good grades or not; my parents didn't notice, didn't care. It didn't matter if you did homework or not. On a typical day, as soon as I got off the bus my mother would have housework for me to do and I would help her with dinner and the dishes. After dinner everyone watched TV until bedtime, There was never any time for homework, I was actually expected to do it at school. I could do it at home if I wanted to, but since we lived in a small house, if I did, it would have to be in the midst of the noise from the TV.

At some time another participant refers to school as a place to escape to, where she could be a different person. That was very true for me in high school, and it may have been even in elementary school, since I remember being absolutely unwilling to miss a day of school; even when I was in the 2nd or 3rd grade I'd scream and cry and generally have a fit.

This "different person" that I became in high school also had a different family! I didn't exactly lie about what was going on at home, but when I talked about my parents I presented them and my home situation as a lot better than they actually were.

Let me say a few things about my teenage depression. First, it was never recognized as anything psychologically important (by my family or by the school). I believe I had a real objective reason for being so depressed—I had to face a reality that WAS depressing. I was constantly being jolted out of my "fantasy" in which I would have a wonderful future full of career and personal success, by admonitions to "face reality," face a reality in which I would never have any of these things, in which I would spend my life having babies and helping to scratch out a living by doing farm labor, Spend my life never having anything, material or otherwise. It was enough to be suicidal about, and maybe the only reason I didn't do away with myself was that I didn't completely believe it. Without reason for having it, I still had a little hope.

It may be also that this explains a little about your observation that your participants saw their achievement "as being completely dependent on their own abilities." I don't think I could have had hope if I hadn't believed at least a little that I had the ability in myself to make my life what I wanted it to be, It was certainly clear to me, at least as far back as high school, that I could not count on anyone else to do anything for me, and that if I wanted something, it was up to me. My parents had opted out, even before I was born. They'd never done anything for the older children; their attitudes were that all of us children owed them for "bringing us into the world." Also, even though school had been a refuge for me, I realize now that the educational system had opted out too. There was never any plan for me in high school that included college. I received no academic counseling; no one ever said, "Take this elective because it will help to get you into college"; nor did anyone ask (until it was too late) whether I was even interested in college. In their (perhaps unthinking) assessment, I was going to be one of those who fell by the wayside. The school was accustomed to losing students from the 7th or 8th grade on, and these were mostly students with my kind of background.

I don't know how I would have reacted if a teacher had noticed that I was depressed. Another participant said she would have been mortified; at first, I thought, "Me, too." But I don't know. I didn't tell anyone how I felt or why. I think I didn't want them to say "so, that's really the way your future looks," and I thought they might. In the 1950s, I don't think teenage depression was considered to be a problem. So I'm not sure that they would have been helpful if I had told a teacher or someone at school.

(3) At one time you ask, "Do children need intervention?" The answer is yes. However, I'm not sure any intervention was available to me, given the insidious nature of my abuse at home. Even if it was, I didn't know it was, and I didn't know how to ask the questions to get it.

At the time, I had no idea that there was anything wrong with my mother or that my family might be dysfunctional. She had a way of defining things as my fault, and I had a way of believing her. She was needful and I felt responsible for making her life better. I learned that there were certain ways I could do this, although these were things that I didn't like, such as staying home from school and doing housework. For about a year once, she kept me out of school every Thursday to help her do the laundry. I was honest about this at school, and it became something of a joke. Everyone learned not to expect me on Thursday. I don't think anyone ever said anything to her about this, such as "Do the laundry yourself," or "Do the laundry on Saturday." It didn't occur to me until many years later that there was anything wrong with this and that someone might have intervened.

(4) I think in these early years I would have appreciated help. But I didn't get much, and maybe this was part of the reason I developed (as you say) such a high level of maturity and independence at an early age. Almost never has anyone else taken care of me. In fact, as it was with my mother, it is usually the other way around. From the time I was 10 years old I was earning my own school money (for clothes and supplies). The minute I got out of high school I got a job and started supporting my mother and brothers. When I married the first time, I always worked. I had the stable job while my husband flitted from job to job. I also supported us while he went to college. Needless to say, I supported myself when I started college; didn't even ask my family or my ex-husband.

I couldn't ask for certain kinds of help such as academic counseling or career guidance because it felt like I would be admitting that those who had assessed me as incapable of succeeding in college were right. As other of your participants said, I had to prove that I could do everything myself. Admitting to any neediness would push me over into an extreme position of admitting to my own incompetence, which I didn't dare do.

(5) You also talked about perfectionism. I think I agree with your assessment, although I don't know how much of a perfectionist I am. This characteristic seems to have varied over my lifetime. There was a change in me in high school that wasn't true before and hasn't been since. I started being satisfied with Cs. In elementary school, I wasn't. I remember the first C; it was in the 5th grade; I think it came out on my report card. I fretted all the way home, and worked up this great story to explain to my family why I got this grade. But I needn't have bothered because when I got there no one even noticed that I had the C, or if they did, they didn't care. Later on, when I was being kept out for the first six weeks of the year, I didn't need to make a story. Anyway it became pointless to worry about grades. The absence period mostly couldn't be made up fully and I would get Ds and Fs to start out. Two years (in the 8th and 9th grades, I think) my sister intervened in this absence pattern by having me stay with her, where I could attend the first six weeks (in summer prior to harvest) of a split term.

(6) In college and grad school, I was in control, and I started to be concerned about getting good grades again. Highly concerned, in fact. My reaction to high school was like that of the other participants, but it was not at the college level, and I think I can tell you why. I didn't start college until six years after high school, until after I was out of my mother's home, until after I was divorced, and until after I was no longer financially responsible for anyone other than myself. During that period, my interest in education skyrocketed, particularly as the only viable route to a career and the good life. This came as a flash of insight one day at my (secretarial) job: I saw myself at age 45 sitting at the same desk, doing the same work, putting in time, letting my life drain away. This jolted me, and I decided then that I had to change this picture and that I would do it myself. Talk about motivation. I had it. But also I found that the community college was wonderful, so personally rewarding, so interesting, so stimulating. I loved it. It was fun, even more than elementary school had been. Later college and graduate school were this way, too. High school was the anomaly.

My high school experience did take its toll on me when I first began college. For one thing, I had heard so much from family and peers implying that I didn't have what it takes to succeed in college that I was very afraid first that I wouldn't be admitted and second that I wouldn't succeed. But in those early days of college I achieved way more than I expected, certainly enough to encourage me.

(7) There was another disadvantage that appeared in my early college experience. I don' t think I told you about this. You may not have asked me, since I am a native English speaker, and one would not expect a language problem. But I had one; it was a pronounced southern accent. I guess I sounded like a hillbilly; everyone certainly treated me like I was. (Let me remind you that I moved from Arkansas to Texas, and then to California, where I started college.) I learned that if I expected anyone to treat me seriously and as anything other than ignorant, I had to get rid of the accent. So I did; over a period of two or three years I worked on my speech and finally dropped the accent. This was the beginning of my hiding my background, for I discovered that the snickering that I heard in response to my speech was actually because of what people thought it signified, that is, a low-class background. So I dropped the accent and the background.

Let me say again that I really appreciate your doing this study, and I m glad you included me. If I can be of further help, just let me know.

Sincerely yours,

Helen

Bibliography

American Association of University Women (AAUW) Educational Foundation. (1992). *How Schools Shortchange Girls.* Washington, DC: AAUW Foundation.

Baldwin, A. F. (1985). *Identification and Programming for Black Children.* Paper presented at the Annual Convention of the Council for Exceptional Children. Sixty-third, Anaheim, CA, April 15-19. (ERIC Document Reproduction Service No. ED 261 495)

Bartolomé, L. I. (1994). Beyond the methods fetish: Toward a humanizing pedagogy. *Harvard Educational Review, 64*(2): 173-194.

Basow, S. A., & Silberg, N. T. (1987). Student evaluations of college professors: Are female and male professors rated differently? *Journal of Educational Psychology, 79*(3): 308-314.

Belenky, M. F., Clinchy, B. M., Goldberger, N., & Tarule, J. (1986). *Women's Ways of Knowing: The Development of Self, Voice and Mind.* New York: Basic Books.

Bempechat, J., & Ginsburg, H. P. (1989). *Underachievement and Educational Disadvantage: The Home and School Experience of At-Risk Youth.* Washington, DC: Office of Educational Research and Improvement (ED). (ERIC Document Reproduction Service No. ED 315 485)

Bock, D. R., & Moore, E. (1986). *Advantage and Disadvantage: A Profile of American Youth.* Hillsdale, NJ: Lawrence Erlbaum Associates.

Caffarella, R. S., & Olson, S. K. (1993). Psychological development of women: A critical review of the literature. *Adult Education Quarterly, 43*(3): 125-151.

Caplan, P. J. (1994). *Lifting a Ton of Feathers: A Woman's Guide to Surviving in the Academic World.* Toronto, Canada: University of Toronto Press.

Carnoy, M., & Levin, H. M. (1986). Educational reform and class conflict. *Journal of Education, 168*(1): 35-46.

Carroll, H. A. (1940). *Genius in the Making.* New York: McGraw-Hill.

Chase, G. (1990). Perhaps we need just say yes. *Journal of Education, 172*(1): 29-37.

Chodorow, N. (1974). Family structure and feminine personality. In M. Z. Rosaldo & L. Lamphere (Eds.), *Women, Culture and Society* (pp. 43-66). Stanford, CA: Stanford University Press.

Clance, P. (1985). *The Impostor Phenomenon.* Atlanta, GA: Peachtree.

Clark, R. (1983). *Family Life and School Achievement: Why Poor Black Children Succeed or Fail.* Chicago, IL: University of Chicago Press.

Clinchy, B. M., Belenky, M. F., Goldberger, N., & Tarule, J. M. (1985). Connected education for women. *Journal of Education, 167*(3): 28-45.

Crosby, F., Pufall, A., Snyder, R., O'Connell, M., & Whalen, P. (1989). The denial of personal disadvantage among you, me, and all the other ostriches. In M. Crawford and M. Gentry (Eds.) *Gender and Thought: Psychological Perspectives* (pp. 79-99). New York: Springer-Verlag.

Daubman, K. A., Heatherington, L., & Ahn, A. (1992). Gender and the self-presentation of academic achievement. *Sex Roles: A Journal of Research, 27*(3/4): 187-204.

Deschamp, P., & Robson, G. (1984). Identifying gifted disadvantaged students: Issues pertinent to system-level screening procedures for the identification of gifted children. *Gifted Education International, 2*(2): 92-99.

Edwards, E. D., Edwards, M. E., Daines, G. M., & Reed, S. M. (1984). Modeling: An important ingredient in higher education for American Indian women students. *Journal of National Association of Women Deans, Administrators and Counselors, 48*(1): 31-35.

Fagenson, E. A. (1992). Mentoring: Who needs it? A comparison of protégés' and nonprotégés' needs for power, achievement, affiliation, and autonomy. *Journal of Vocational Behavior, 41*(1): 48-60.

Fantini, M., & Weinstein, G. (1968). *The Disadvantaged: Challenge to Education.* New York: Harper and Row.

Ferree, G. (1985). The epistemology of knowing how students feel. *American Journal of Education, 93*(2): 240-251.

Fisher-McCanne, L. P., McCanne, T. R., & Keating, L. (1980). The impact of academic environment and student services on the academic progress of women. *Journal of College Student Personnel, 21*(1): 74-80.

Flores, J. (1988). *Chicana Doctoral Students: Another Look at Educational Equity.* Also in Garcia, H. S., & Ghavez, R. *Ethnolinguistic Issues in Education* (1988). (ERIC Document Reproduction Service No. ED 316 041).

Fordham, S., & Ogbu, J. U. (1986). Black students' school success: Coping with the "burden of 'acting white.'" *The Urban Review, 18*(3): 176-206.

Freire, P. (1970). *The Pedagogy of the Oppressed.* New York: Continuum.

French, J. L., & Murphy, J. P. (1983). Parenting of gifted children: A two-edged sword. *Roeper Review, 5*(3): 36-37.

Frierson, E. D. (1965). Upper and lower status gifted children: A study of differences. *Exceptional Children, October (32):* 83-89.

Furumoto, L. (1980). Biographies of eminent women in psychology: Models for achievement. *Psychology of Women Quarterly, 5*(1): 55-139.

Gandara, P. (1982). Passing through the eye of the needle: High-achieving Chicanas. *Hispanic Journal of Behavioral Sciences, 4*(2): 167-179.

Gandara, P. (1995). *Over the Ivy Walls: The Educational Mobility of Low-Income Chicanos.* Albany, NY: State University of New York Press.

Gardner, H. (1983). *Frames of Mind: The Theory of Multiple Intelligences.* New York: Basic Books.

Garmezy, N. (1991). Resiliency and vulnerability to adverse developmental outcomes associated with poverty. *American Behavioral Scientist, 34*(4): 416-430.

Gilligan, C. (1982). *In a Different Voice.* Cambridge, MA: Harvard University Press.

Goleman, D. (1995). *Emotional Intelligence: Why Can It Matter More than IQ?* New York: Bantam Books.

Gotwalt, N., & Towns, K. (1986). Rare as they are, women at the top can teach us all. *The Executive Educator, 8*(12): 13-29.

Gould, R. L. (1978). *Growth and Change in Adult Life.* New York: Simon and Schuster.

Hayes, E. R., & Smith, L. (1994). Women in adult education: An analysis of perspectives in major journals. *Adult Education Quarterly, 44*(4): 201-219.

Hearn, J. C., & Olzark, S. (1981). The role of college major departments in the reproduction of sexual inequality. *Sociology of Education, 54*(3): 195-205.

Hirsch, E. D. (1996). *The Schools We Need and Why Ee Don't Have Them.* New York: Doubleday.

Hobson-Smith, C. (1982). Black female achievers in academe. *Journal of Negro Education , 51*(3): 318-341.

Hollingsworth, S. (1994). *Teacher Research and Urban Literacy Education. Lessons and Conversations in a Feminist Key.* New York: Teachers College Press.

Jussim, L. (1993). Self-fulfilling prophecies: A theoretical and integrative review. *Psychological Review, 93*(4): 429-445.

Kanoy, K. W., Wester, J., & Latta, M. (1990). Understanding differences between high- and low-achieving women: Implications for effective teaching and placement. *Journal of College Student Development, 31*(2): 133-140.

Knowles, M. S. (1970). *The Modern Practice of Adult Education: Andragogy versus Pedagogy.* New York: Association Press.

LePage, P. (1991). When do education students talk about personal experience? An analysis of classroom discourse. *College Student Journal, 28*(2): 179-191.

Levin, H. M. (1985). *The State Youth Initiatives Project. The Educationally Disadvantaged: A National Crisis.* Philadelphia, PA: Public/Private Ventures. (ERIC Document Reproduction No. ED 304 496)

Levin, H. M. (1987). Accelerated Schools for Disadvantaged Students. *Leadership, 44*(6): 19-21.

Levine, A., & Nidiffer, J. (1996). *Beating the Odds: How the Poor Get to College.* San Francisco, CA: Jossey Bass.

Lincoln, Y. S. (1988). Naturalistic Inquiry: Politics and implications for special education. *Proceedings of the Research in Education of the Handicapped Project Director's Meeting.* Washington, DC, July 10-12. (ERIC Document Reproduction No. ED 212 773)

Lincoln, Y. S., & Guba, E. G. (1985). *Naturalistic Inquiry.* Newbury Park, CA: Sage.

Marshall, C., & Rossman, G. (1989). *Designing Qualitative Research.* Newbury Park, CA: Sage.

Marsick, V. J. (1985). *Working with the Adult Learners in Higher Education: Going against Internalized Norms.* Paper presented at the Conference of the American Association for Adult and Continuing Education. Milwaukee, WI, Nov. 6-10. (ERIC Document Reproduction Service No. ED 264 388)

Martin, D., Harrison, D., & Dinitto, D. (1983). Hierarchical organizations: A multilevel analysis of problems and prospects. *The Journal of Applied Behavior Science, 19:* 19-33.

McElroy-Johnson, B. (1993). Giving voice to the voiceless. *Harvard Educational Review, 63*(1): 85-104.

Meyers, D. G. (1993). *Social Psychology.* 4th edition. New York: McGraw-Hill.

Noddings, N. (1992). *The Challenge to Care in Schools.* New York: Teachers College Press.

Oakes, J. (1985). *Keeping Track: How Schools Structure Inequality.* New Haven: Yale University Press.

O'Connell, A. N., & Russo, N. F. (1980). Models for achievement: Eminent women in psychology. *Psychology of Women Quarterly, 5*(1): 6-54.

Ogbu, J. (1990). Understanding diversity, summary comments. *Education and Urban Society, 22* (4): 425-429.

Orenstein, P. (1994). *School Girls: Young Women, Self-esteem and the Confidence Gap.* New York: Doubleday.

Patton, M. Q. (1990). *Qualitative evaluation and research methods.* Newbury Park, CA: Sage.

Poplin, M. S., & Stone, S. (1992). Paradigm shifts in instructional strategies: From reductionism to holistic constructivism. In W. Stainback and S. Stainback (Eds.), *Controversial Issues Confronting Special Education.* (pp. 153-179). Boston, MA: Allyn and Bacon.

Range, J. A. (1990). The IP (Impostor Phenomenon) and women in theology. In L. B. Welch (Ed.), *Women in Higher Education: Challenges and Changes* (pp. 46-56). New York: Praeger.

Rhodes, W. A., & Brown, W. K. (1991). *Why Some Children Succeed Despite the Odds.* New York: Praeger.

Rivera, J,, & Poplin, M. (1995). Multicultural, critical, feminine and constructive pedagogies seen through the lives of youth: A call for the revisioning of these and beyond: Toward a pedagogy for the next century. In C, E. Sleeter and P. L. McLaren (Eds.), *Multicultural Education, Critical Pedagogy, and the Politics of Difference* (pp. 221-244). New York: State University of New York Press.

Rodrigues, R. (1990). *Hunger of Memory: The Education of Richard Rodriguez.* New York: Bantam Books.

Rutter, M. (1979). *Fifteen Thousand Hours.* Cambridge, MA: Harvard University Press.

Saarni, C. (1979). *When NOT to Show What You Feel: Children's Understanding of Relations between Emotional Experiences and Expressive Behavior.* Paper presented at the Biannual Meeting of the Society for Research in Child Development. San Francisco, CA, March 15-18. Chicago, IL: Spencer Foundation. (ERIC Document Reproduction Service No. ED 171 396)

Sadker, M., & Sadker, D. (1994). *Failing at Fairness: How America's Schools Cheat Girls.* New York: Charles Scribner's Sons.

Saul, J. R. (1992). Women speak about their learning experiences in higher education. *Initiatives, 55*(1): 43-51.

Scandura, T. A. (1992). Mentorship and career mobility: An empirical investigation. *Journal of Organizational Behavior, 13*(2): 169-174.

Schappell, M. P. (1990). The effect of attitudinal similarity and gender on performance ratings in mentor-mentee dyads. Ph.D. Dissertation, George Washington University. Abstract in *Dissertation Abstracts International, 51*(5-B): 2659.

Sheehan, E. P., McMenamin, N., & McDevit, T. M. (1992). Learning styles of traditional and nontraditional university students. *College Student Journal, 26*(4): 486-490.

Skinner, E. F., & Richardson, R. (1988). Making it in a majority university. *Change, 20*(3): 37-42.

Slavin, R. E., & Madden, N. A. (1989). What works for students at-risk: A research synthesis. *Leadership, 46*(5): 4-13.

Sockett, H. (1993). *The Moral Base for Teacher Professionalism.* New York: Teachers College Press.

Summers-Ewing, D. (1994). *Mentoring: A Vital Ingredient for Career Success.* Los Angeles, CA: American Psychological Association. (ERIC Document Reproduction Service No. ED 378 519)

Tarule, J. M. (1988). Voices of returning women: Ways of knowing. In L. H. Lewis (Ed.), *Addressing the Needs of Returning Women: New Directions for Continuing Education* (pp. 19-33). San Francisco, CA: Jossey-Bass.

Taylor, A. (1990). *Integrating Critical Thinking and Creative Thinking in the Cooperative Learning Model. Implications for Addressing the Frame of Reference for these Two Distinct Processes.* Paper presented at the National Conference on Cooperative Learning. Baltimore, MD. (ERIC Document Reproduction Service No. ED 032- 642)

Terenzini, P. T., Rendon, L. I., Upcraft, M. L., Millar, S. B., Allison, K. W., Gregg, P. L., & Jalomo, R. (1993). The transition to college: Diverse students, diverse stories. *Research in Higher Education, 35*(1): 57-73.

Turban, D. B., & Dougherty, T. W. (1994). Role of protégé personality in receipt of mentoring and career success. *Academy of Management Journal, 37*(3): 688-702.

Wells, A. (1989). *The Disadvantaged: Paths to Success.* NCEE Brief Number 3. National Center on Education and Employment, New York. (ERIC Document Reproduction Service No. ED 309 252)

Werner, E. E., & Smith, R. (1983). *Vulnerable but Invincible.* New York: McGraw-Hill.

Wilson, W. J. (1987). *The Truly Disadvantaged: The Inner City, the Underclass, and Public Policy.* Chicago, IL: University of Chicago Press.

Wilson, K. L., & Boldizar, J. P. (1990). Gender segregation in higher education: Effects of aspirations, mathematics achievement, and income. *Sociology of Education, 63*(1): 62-74.

Wyche, K. F., & Graves, S. B. (1992). Minority women in academia. *Psychology of Women Quarterly, 16*(4): 429-437.

Index

About the Author

PAMELA LePAGE-LEES is an Assistant Professor in a School-Based Master's Program for teachers at the Institute for Educational Transformation (IET) at the George Mason University. Prior to that, she served as a Visiting Assistant Professor at The George Washington University in Washington, D. C. She has also taught in the Education Departments at San Diego State University and San Francisco State University. Her research focuses on understanding the special learning needs of women, nontraditional college students and teachers.